"This is the clearest, most artic [tation] of help for worry and Although intended for women, it will be quite helpful to women and men alike who seek to overcome chronic worry. The process of analyzing "worry spirals" and intervening with coping strategies at the earliest possible moment was particularly useful. I will recommend this book to my clients with generalized anxiety disorder (GAD.)"

—*Edmund J. Bourne, Ph.D., author of* The Anxiety and Phobia Workbook

"This is the best book I have seen on ways to deal with chronic worry. The strategies are based on the latest research regarding the nature and treatment of worry, and the concepts and strategies are explained in a straightforward, easy-to-understand manner. I highly recommend this book to any woman who worries too much, to any mental health professional who treats worry, and even to men who worry more than they want to!

—*Martin M. Antony, Ph.D., ABPP, director of the Anxiety Treatment and Research Centre at St. Joseph's Healthcare and professor in the Department of Psychiatry and Behavioural Neurosciences at McMaster University, both in Hamilton, ON, Canada*

"Given the greater likelihood that a woman will suffer from chronic anxiety, it is refreshing to see a book that focuses solely on the struggles of women who worry too much. Hazlett-Stevens draws from the most efficacious techniques available and translates them for the reader so that they are practical, easy to understand, and readily useable. This book is sure to provide women who worry with the tools they need to worry less and lead fuller, more valued lives."

—*Douglas S. Mennin, Ph.D., assistant professor of psychology and director of the Yale Anxiety and Mood Services at Yale University, New Haven, CT*

women who worry too much

WITHDRAWN

How to Stop Worry & Anxiety from Ruining Relationships, Work & Fun

Holly Hazlett-Stevens, Ph.D.

New Harbinger Publications, Inc.

152.46

Hazlett-Stevens Publisher's Note

This publication is designed to provide accurate and authoritative information in regard to the subject matter covered. It is sold with the understanding that the publisher is not engaged in rendering psychological, financial, legal, or other professional services. If expert assistance or counseling is needed, the services of a competent professional should be sought.

Distributed in Canada by Raincoast Books.

Copyright © 2005 by Holly Hazlett-Stevens
New Harbinger Publications, Inc.
5674 Shattuck Avenue
Oakland, CA 94609

Cover design by Amy Shoup; Text design by Michele Waters-Kermes; Acquired by Tesilya Hanauer; Edited by Jasmine Star

ISBN 1-57224-412-7 Paperback

New Harbinger Publications' Web site address: www.newharbinger.com

Library of Congress Cataloging-in-Publication Data

Hazlett-Stevens, Holly.
  Women who worry too much : how to stop worry and anxiety from ruining relationships, work, and fun / Holly Hazlett-Stevens.
      p. cm.
  Includes bibliographical references.
  ISBN 1-57224-412-7
  1. Worry. 2. Women—Psychology. I. Title.
  BF575.W8H39 2005
  152.4'6—dc22
                                  2005014382

07   06   05

10   9   8   7   6   5   4   3   2   1

First printing

For Tom,
a wonderful mentor and extraordinary human being

Contents

Acknowledgments

The information and exercises contained in this book are based on the research, clinical experience, and theoretical work of many experts. Several psychological researchers have devoted their careers to understanding worry and anxiety and how to overcome them. This book wouldn't be possible without their invaluable contributions. Although a complete list of names isn't feasible, my thinking about worry has been largely influenced by the work and ideas of Thomas Borkovec, Michelle Newman, Louis Castonguay, Robert Ladouceur, Michel Dugas, Mark Freeston, David Barlow, Michelle Craske, Graham Davey, Adrian Wells, Gillian Butler, Lars-Göran Öst, Douglas Bernstein, Richard Heimberg, Lizabeth Roemer, and Susan Orsillo.

I am eternally grateful to the many psychologists who have mentored and supervised me throughout my training. I am especially indebted to Tom Borkovec and Michelle Craske for all of their wisdom, personal encouragement, and professional support they have shared with me over the years.

I would also like to thank my editors at New Harbinger, Tesilya Hanauer and Heather Mitchener, for all of their hard work and helpful feedback on drafts of the chapters. A special thanks to Tesilya for coming up with the concept and title for the book—this work would not have come about without her vision. I'm also grateful to Michelle Craske and Najwa Chowdhury for their excellent introduction and to Jasmine Star for her wonderful copyediting.

Thanks to my husband, Chris, for your unwavering love and support.

And finally, I'd like to thank all of the worriers I've met in my personal and professional life who have shared their struggles and triumphs with me. Our knowledge of worry is not complete without an understanding of the human experience behind it, no matter how much academic theory and research might be available.

INTRODUCTION

Why Are Women Anxious and Worried More Often Than Men?

MICHELLE G. CRASKE, PH.D.
& NAJWA CHOWDHURY, BS
Department of Psychology,
University of California, Los Angeles

Did you know that women are twice as likely as men to develop an anxiety disorder? The reasons for this difference between the sexes are not entirely clear, but in this introduction we'll explore what causes anxiety disorders, why women struggle with worry and anxiety more than men, and how a woman's biology and past experiences might make her more prone to an anxiety disorder.

WHAT CAUSES ANXIETY DISORDERS?

Anxiety disorders and other forms of emotional distress, such as depression, are believed to share a common underlying thread. All of these conditions seem to share a general tendency to feel unpleasant feelings. In other words, some people are naturally more prone to experiencing negative emotions such as fear, anxiety, and sadness. This personality trait is known as *negative affectivity.* On its own, this tendency doesn't necessarily lead to emotional problems. But imagine if someone with this tendency has a series of experiences that teach him or her to see some aspect of himself or herself or the outside world as dangerous. He or she would soon become even more likely to struggle with anxiety, to view the world as unsafe, and to react to situations by withdrawing from them or avoiding them altogether. The stronger a person's initial negative affectivity and the more that person views his or her surroundings as threatening, the greater the chances anxiety will develop across a number of situations.

Anxiety often involves *hypervigilance,* in which a person pays too much attention to minor details, looking for sources of threat. When the mind is hypervigilant, the body's physiology also changes. These physical changes keep the mind even more on the lookout for danger. The person becomes increasingly likely to judge events and his or her surroundings as dangerous and reacts by avoiding these things as much as possible. You can see how these factors work together to fuel anxiety in a self-perpetuating way.

How does a person develop anxiety in response to one particular type of situation or object over others? This is where specific life experiences come in. Let's take the example of a fear of dogs. Someone may become afraid of dogs following a traumatic experience of being attacked by a dog. Or the person may have a *vicarious* experience in which he or she witnesses someone else having a traumatic experience with a dog or simply witnesses someone responding to a dog with intense fear. A person can also become afraid of dogs by being told that dogs are dangerous and scary, and need to be avoided. Any one of these experiences can boost a person's view that a particular object or situation, such as a dog, poses a real threat. What's more, a person prone to negative affectivity will probably experience a greater impact from these events than someone without such an emotional tendency.

A person's entire history of life experiences is also important. For example, if attacked by a dog, someone with several years of fond memories with dogs is less likely to develop a fear of dogs than a person who has little previous experience with dogs. General life experiences matter too. People who have enjoyed many successful experiences and developed a strong sense of control over their life may be less vulnerable to anxiety than people without a strong sense of control. Finally, anxiety itself can make a person even more vulnerable to further anxiety and distress, especially when the experience of anxiety feels unpredictable or uncontrollable.

WHEN DO ANXIETY DISORDERS DEVELOP?

You might be surprised to learn that, in childhood, girls are no more anxious than boys. But girls become much more prone to anxiety and worry than boys do as they approach puberty and face adolescence. In one research study, McGee and colleagues (1992) followed a large group of girls and boys for several years, looking for a severe form of worry and anxiety called *generalized anxiety disorder*. Although they found no gender differences at all when the children were eleven years old, by the time they reached adolescence, the number of girls suffering from this serious condition was six times greater than the number of boys. What's more, anxious young girls are at a heightened risk for future anxiety difficulties when they reach adolescence, and girls who are anxious during adolescence have a heightened risk of suffering from anxiety in early adulthood. As you can see, adolescence through early adulthood is quite a vulnerable time for women to develop an anxiety disorder. Women are also especially likely to develop anxiety disorders during middle age, usually between the ages of forty-five to sixty-four (Offord et al. 1996).

Even though there's an undeniable difference between women and men in the occurrence of anxiety disorders, the exact reason for this disparity remains a mystery. On a related note, women are more likely than men to become depressed. This may be partially explained by women's higher rates of anxiety, because anxiety often leads to depression.

WHAT PUTS WOMEN AT A GREATER RISK FOR ANXIETY DISORDERS?

Although we don't have all the answers to why women have a greater risk of developing anxiety disorders, several known differences between men and women help explain this phenomenon. These include differences in how boys and girls are raised, women's natural tendency to experience certain emotions more intensely than men, and biological differences in how women and men respond to stress.

Parenting Practices and Gender Roles

Different styles of parenting for boys versus girls can be seen in the very first few months of life. New mothers appear more in tune with their sons' signals and needs than their daughters', perhaps because their sons express greater emotional needs. Whatever the reason for this difference in parenting, tuning into an infant's subtle signs and expressions can be very important to childhood development. This is when children first learn how predictable and controllable their world and their own emotions are. A sense of predictability and control is critical to the ability to manage emotional arousal and the degree to which distress is experienced (Craske 2003). However, there has been no direct study of the relationship between how tuned in parents are to their infants and a child's proneness to anxiety disorders.

Different behaviors are rewarded for boys versus girls throughout childhood. Typically, parents and others encourage boys to be more assertive, active, and independent. On the other hand, anxious and avoidant behaviors are more often reinforced for girls. Because traits like shyness and anxiety are less accepted in boys than girls, anxious boys may be encouraged to overcome their fears. But anxious girls are often rewarded for their anxiety, even if this is done unintentionally.

Parents or other important adults sometimes treat boys and girls differently because they believe that boys are more capable. As a result, boys are encouraged to face challenges in a wide variety of situations, in the process developing skills that lead to success, such as coping strategies and persistence. In addition, through facing challenges, boys are more likely than girls to accumulate positive experiences that buffer them from later negative experiences. Boys are therefore likely to perceive themselves as stronger, more dominant, and more in control than girls (Ohannessian et al. 1999). This difference continues throughout adolescence and adulthood.

Girls aren't only socialized to be less assertive and independent than boys; they're also encouraged to be more sociable and empathic. Women, especially those who see themselves as very feminine, tend to express empathy toward others more than men. This type of social "training" fits with women's greater sensitivity to facial expressions. It also probably leaves women more vulnerable to developing specific fears if they witness someone else acting afraid, as women are better at detecting threat through others' facial expressions.

The Tendency to Feel Unpleasant Feelings

It's possible that women are more vulnerable to developing anxiety and depressive disorders because they tend to experience greater negative affectivity, that general tendency to experience negative emotions such as fear, anxiety, and sadness. In a research study conducted by Arcus and Kagan (1995), girls were more inhibited and showed greater negative affectivity than boys beginning around the age of two. This is the same time when *socialization*—learning how to behave from other people in the child's environment—is first seen for each gender. The difference between the sexes in negative affectivity continues to increase from childhood through adolescence, with boys showing no change while girls show a clear rise in this trait. Because women are more prone to negative affectivity, women are believed to be at a greater risk for picking up on threats, learning to fear certain things, and remaining more emotionally reactive to unpleasant events.

In addition to the gender gap in negative affectivity, which is found among many populations around the world (Lynn and Martin 1997), women react to facial expressions more than men do. This heightened sensitivity to facial expressions helps explain why women learn to fear things more often than men. That's because simply watching someone else react to something with fear is a common way people become afraid of certain things.

Research also shows that women worry and *ruminate*, or think things over, more than men. Sometimes, reflecting about things helps us plan ahead and carefully examine important choices in life. But both worry and rumination can get in the way of active problem solving, and both can lead to ongoing feelings of distress. Worry seems to get triggered by uncertainty about possible threats off in the future. Too much worry usually reflects that the person sees a wide range of potential problems and disasters on the horizon.

Women are also more likely than men to focus on negative aspects of themselves. This *negative self-focus* then creates more feelings of distress and bad mood (Mor and Winquist 2002). Other research suggests that women are more in tune with their internal emotional state than men tend to be (Pennebaker 2000). Of course it can be beneficial to tune into your emotional state, allowing you to discover what's really best for you. But the more intensely a person experiences uncomfortable internal emotional responses, the more afraid they are likely to become. So women's heightened internal awareness may create more fear and anxiety.

Not only do women have a greater awareness of their internal experience, they are also less accurate in judging what's actually happening inside. Women rely on what's happening around them to determine how they feel inside more than men do (Pennebaker and Roberts 1992). This makes sense because women are more sensitive to others' facial expressions—a common place people look to make judgments about surrounding danger and their own emotional state. Certainly it's useful to be sensitive to other people's feelings: this allows us to form close, caring relationships and enjoy intimacy with others. But when people rely too heavily on the external situation and others' reactions to judge how they feel, they become less able to read their own internal sensations accurately. This can lead to a lot of anxiety, often accompanied by the tendency to jump to conclusions.

If men are more likely to rely on their internal signals and read them accurately to judge their emotional state, they're more able to discriminate between what is and is not dangerous. For women, several influences combine to leave them less able to make these discriminations, so they respond with anxiety across a wider variety of situations. These influences include worry, negative self-focus, and relying too much on outside details to judge what they feel inside, while also experiencing their emotions more intensely.

Women are no more likely to experience traumatic life events than men are. In fact, women are exposed to fewer traumas overall. So the number of major adversities doesn't seem to account for the higher rates of anxiety disorders in women. On the other hand, women are more prone to emotional distress following a major trauma or life crisis. This increased emotional reactivity is likely to contribute to an ongoing cycle of distress and strong emotional reactions to future stress, eventually leaving women more vulnerable to anxiety disorders.

Fight-or-Flight vs. Tend-and-Befriend

The study of physiology and behavior shows that women have a general tendency to respond to situations with anxiety. This research is very intriguing because it helps explain how women and men may have evolved differently over the course of human history. Important differences between the sexes have been found when looking at their responses to immediate stress. Both men and women experience the *fight-or-flight response* when faced with a stressful situation. During this response, many physiological changes occur within the body. For example, the heart beats faster and adrenaline is released. These bodily responses serve to prepare the body to either fight a threat or flee from the dangerous situation. But this response evolved at a time when humans lived in a very different environment than the one we live in now. That's why this fight-or-flight response is not always an appropriate response to the stress humans experience today.

The difference between women and men is that, in women, certain hormones become active when a sudden stressor occurs. These hormones *downregulate*, or dampen the effects of, the fight-or-flight system. So women show a blunted physiological response to acute stress compared with men. This dampening of the fight-or-flight response is important from the perspective of evolution because it serves to protect the offspring. Instead of fighting or fleeing, a woman's drive during stress is to tend to her children and befriend others for the security of group protection. Importantly, this natural *tend-and-befriend* stress response may reinforce an avoidant way of coping with perceived threats, which can ultimately reinforce anxiety and the perception of threat. In contrast, although men's fight-or-flight response exposes them to more threats, it also gives them the chance to find effective ways of defeating those threats. This is another way that men learn independence and assertiveness.

IN CONCLUSION

In this introduction, we've explored some of the reasons why women are more prone to anxiety and worry than men. Although there are undeniable factors—biological, social, and psychological—that predispose women to heightened anxiety responses, it *is* within your power to overcome anxiety and worry if they're a problem for you. The simple but effective techniques described in this book have helped many people and are supported by scientific research. We wish you the greatest success as you use the strategies in this book to confront your own tendency to worry.

PART I

THE NATURE OF WORRY AND ANXIETY

CHAPTER 1

Fundamentals of Worry

SHARON: WORRIED SICK

Sharon was a worrier. During most of her waking hours, her mind raced with thoughts of what could go wrong at work or with her kids. She was often restless and on edge, not knowing how to slow down long enough to relax. Lately, this constant tension seemed to spill into every area of her life: she was snapping at her husband, kids, and friends; she couldn't concentrate at work; and her sex life was practically nonexistent. Sharon's worry and tension began to take a toll on her body as well. Her stomach was always tied up in knots, her upper back and shoulders ached from constant muscle tension, and she seemed to catch a cold or the flu every time a new bug was going around the office or her children's school. Sharon considered herself lucky if she got even four hours of sleep at night. Most nights she would lie awake in bed for hours before falling asleep, ironically worrying about the fact that she wasn't sleeping!

Eventually, Sharon began to worry about all of this too. She worried about the fact that she worried so much, wondering where this was all heading. *How can I continue to live this way?* she thought. *What if I'm wearing myself down and missing out on the best years of my life?* Sharon felt ashamed and embarrassed by her worry. She also felt helpless, not knowing what else to do. It was as if worry was a dark cloud following her around wherever she went: *What if I don't finish this project by four o'clock? How will I be able to leave work on time to pick up the kids? I'm so exhausted. How am I going to get through another day without any sleep? And what if I get sick again? I can't afford any more time off from work.*

If Sharon's story sounds at all familiar, you are not alone. Many women struggle with worry and anxiety over the course of their lives. And many of them overcome it, learning how to keep anxious thoughts and feelings from invading and running their lives. Perhaps Sharon's story sounds different from or more extreme than the worry you experience. Or maybe worry affects your life in some other way. If so, don't lose hope—this book is for any woman who worries more than she thinks she needs to, regardless of what the worry is about or how many symptoms she experiences.

WHAT IS WORRY?

Although we all know what worry is firsthand, it can be a bit tricky to define. How can you tell when you're worrying as opposed to simply thinking about something? Most people consider it worry when they're thinking negatively or pessimistically about an upcoming situation or when they're second-guessing themselves about something that has already happened. When people worry, they are usually questioning, *What if something goes wrong, or has already gone wrong, and I can't cope with it?* If they keep asking themselves these questions without resolution, they become more and more anxious. For this reason, worry is usually considered to be the thinking component of anxiety. It's what you are saying to yourself when you're anxious, usually in anticipation of some future outcome or event.

You might be reading this book because you consider your worry to be excessive or out of control. But keep in mind that most people worry to some degree from time to time. In fact, our ability to worry at all comes from our natural capacity to plan ahead by thinking into the future. Without this basic human trait, we would hardly be able to function. Imagine having to live your life without being able to think into the future and plan ahead. You would probably find yourself without the groceries you need to make dinner, without clean clothes to wear when you get dressed for work, or running out of gas while driving a long distance.

Another benefit of our ability to think ahead is that it allows us to anticipate and solve potential problems even before they occur. In this case, thinking about the future leads to action that provides a specific solution to a specific problem at hand. For example, imagine you arrive at work one morning and your boss tells you you'll have to work through your lunch hour. But you already have a lunch meeting scheduled with a friend. Realizing that you'll soon be expected in two different places at once presents you with a very specific problem to be solved. Once you've identified the problem, you can start generating possible solutions, weigh them all out, and then act on the best possible choice. You might decide to resolve the situation by telling your boss you already have plans, or by rescheduling your lunch with your friend. In other words, you can effectively solve a specific problem by thinking ahead a few hours and taking action.

On the other hand, worry quickly results if you try to solve vague problems, try to solve problems without solutions, or try to prevent something from happening that probably never will happen. If no specific problem exists or if there are no specific solutions under your control, the whole process falls apart. Instead of lowering your anxiety or stress level by providing a sense of resolution, thinking ahead has only generated more anxiety. This type of thinking is considered worry.

Problem Solving	Worry
Concrete problem	Vague problem
Possible solutions	No specific solutions
Problem resolved after weighing choices	Issue remains unresolved
Thinking ahead leads to action	Thinking ahead leads to anxiety

AWARENESS EXERCISE 1:
Worry vs. Problem Solving

The goal of this exercise is to distinguish between problem solving and worry:

1. Think of a clear, concrete problem that can easily be solved. For example, say it's your turn in the carpool to pick up the kids, but you need to go to a doctor's appointment. Notice how this is a concrete problem that can be solved with a specific course of action.

2. Now think of a worry. Common examples include asking yourself what if you make a wrong decision, fail to achieve something, or disappoint other people. All of these are quite

vague. None of them can be resolved with specific solutions and action.

3. Use the lists above to help you make a distinction between problem solving and worry. Over the next couple of days, tune into your thoughts and see if you can tell when you're worrying and when you're successfully problem solving. Notice how it feels to solve concrete problems effectively compared to getting caught up with worry.

4. If you notice yourself worrying, ask yourself if there is anything specific you can do right at that moment to handle the situation. This can help you shift into problem-solving mode if there is a specific problem at hand that is under your control.

HOW IS WORRY DIFFERENT FROM ANXIETY, FEAR, AND PANIC?

While worry is the specific type of thinking described above, *anxiety* refers to all of the feelings and bodily sensations that go along with worry. Worry is your mind thinking ahead into the future to anticipate possible threats. Anxiety is how your body responds in anticipation of those future threats. One of the most common anxiety symptoms linked to chronic worry is muscle tension. However, more arousing anxiety symptoms, such as your heart racing or feeling short of breath, can happen in anticipation as a specific event or situation grows near.

Fear is the basic emotion you feel when your mind perceives immediate danger. Fear is a very physical emotion because it serves the purpose of protecting you from harm as soon as possible. The automatic physical response that occurs during fear is often called the *fight-or-flight response* because your body is gearing up to attack or to run from the threat. For example, your heart beats faster and stronger to get your blood flowing to large muscles. This delivers the oxygen your muscles need to move your body quickly. Your breathing also speeds up so that more oxygen is available to the body. Increased sweating helps cool the body for physical activity like fighting or running. Unlike worry, fear involves very little thinking. Instead, your body is carrying out a primitive biological program designed to keep you safe from harm.

Some people experience this fight-or-flight fear response in the absence of real danger, an experience called *panic*. People can struggle with both extremes, alternating between worry and panic. Although some of the strategies described in this book can be applied to panic, they're presented in a way most helpful for managing worry. If you're concerned that you might be experiencing panic, you may find some of the resources listed at the back of this book useful.

WHAT CAUSES CHRONIC WORRY?

What makes women prone to worry? There is no simple answer to this question because a combination of different factors seems to be important. You've just read in the introduction why women suffer from anxiety and worry more than men do. Sometimes learning why women experience certain problems more than men leaves women feeling discouraged. They make the mistake of thinking that their gender caused their troubles or that they can't overcome these difficulties because they're female. Men have problems every bit as much as women do; they just tend to struggle with other things. This is also not to say that men don't worry or feel anxious. Most people worry from time to time and some men do face severe and chronic worry.

People often ask whether anxiety and worry are caused by biological factors, such as genes, or by environmental factors, such as childhood experiences. You may have heard of this distinction as the *nature versus nurture controversy*. The problem with this controversy is that *both* types of factors are proving to be very important. What's more, these factors don't simply lead to worry and anxiety independently. Instead, it's how they interact or feed off each other that ultimately makes a person susceptible to symptoms of anxiety and worry.

Have you ever wondered if your worry is genetic? Plenty of research suggests that genes play a role. But worry isn't genetically inherited like genetically caused diseases are. A person's genetic makeup can include a very general tendency to react to situations with a heightened anxiety response. This tendency to experience anxiety and other emotions may or may not lead to problems with worry, anxiety, or depression. Even if a person inherits this genetic makeup—believed to be made up of a combination of several genes, not just one—that person's experiences and environment can prevent him or her from ever having problems with negative emotions and related psychological difficulties. This genetic trait is also very general, or *nonspecific*. That's why inheriting this general emotional tendency can lead to one anxiety disorder in one person, entirely different symptoms of another anxiety disorder in a second person, and depression in still another person.

Genes aren't the only reason people develop the personality traits or *temperament* that make them prone to worry and anxiety. Environmental influences can be quite powerful too. Can you think of any childhood experiences where the world seemed unpredictable and difficult to control? This is the type of experience most often linked to chronic worry. If it happens enough, people learn to perceive the world as dangerous. They might also learn to perceive themselves as unable to control their surroundings and poorly equipped to cope. Extreme trauma, such as recurrent child abuse, is certainly one example. However, much less dramatic experiences can also be crucial. Examples might include caring for a depressed or ill parent as a child; having a parent, teacher, or other caregiver who is inconsistent with punishment or overly critical; or being taunted, bullied, or picked on at school with no way to make the teasing stop.

Overprotective parenting or being around people who react to situations with worry and anxiety may also have an impact. Worry and anxiety run in families not only because of genes, but also because these patterns of reacting can be learned. Many similar experiences can contribute to a sense that the world is a dangerous place, that the future holds many possible threats, and that you'll be unable to handle them.

AWARENESS EXERCISE 2:
Reflect on Your Own Experience

Think back over your own life experiences:

1. Try to identify any experiences over the course of your childhood and adulthood that may have contributed to your tendency to worry. Look for experiences in which you felt that life was too unpredictable, that you were in over your head, or that you couldn't control what was happening.

2. Ask yourself the following questions:

- How might these past experiences influence the way you see yourself, other people, and the world now?

- What expectations do you carry into current situations and interactions with people based on your past experiences?

- How might your tendency to experience anxiety and other negative emotions impact the way you interpret your current environment?

- How might a tendency to view the future as threatening and yourself as unable to cope impact your behavior in certain situations?

WOMEN AND WORRY

What do women usually worry about? Although we don't really know how women's worry differs from men's, people tend to worry about their families and personal relationships most often. Other common topics include work or school, finances, and physical health or safety. Chronic worriers also worry about little things. Life's everyday hassles, such as getting the car repaired, and minor concerns, such as arriving on time for an appointment, are likely to trigger the worry process for them. People who worry a lot also express fears of failure, inadequacy, and incompetence in their worry more than people who don't worry very much.

Women tend to struggle with worry more than men do. Women sometimes score higher than men on pencil-and-paper worry questionnaires (Meyer et al. 1990). Researchers studying *generalized anxiety disorder*, in which people experience an extreme form of excessive and uncontrollable worry along with certain chronic anxiety symptoms, found that over 5 percent of Americans suffer from this chronic anxiety disorder at some point during their lifetime (Wittchen et al. 1994). Women were twice as likely as men to have this disorder. The Anxiety Disorders Association of America (2003) estimates that four million American adults suffer from generalized anxiety disorder. This means about 2.6 million women in the United States alone struggle with worry in its most severe form.

Many other women suffer from chronic worry without a diagnosis of generalized anxiety disorder. Important survey results from Pennsylvania State University showed that 28 percent of college students were experiencing severe levels of excessive and uncontrollable worry even though only 6 percent had the symptoms necessary for a diagnosis of generalized anxiety disorder (Ruscio 2002). Chronic worry can compromise the immune system and is sometimes associated with physical problems such as gastrointestinal distress. This might explain why people with generalized anxiety disorder visit their medical doctors more often than people without anxiety or depression conditions.

Chronic worry often leads to anxiety symptoms, such as ongoing muscle tension, tension headaches, and trouble falling or staying asleep. Worrying much of the time also leads to irritability and difficulty concentrating. The very process of worry takes your mind away from the present moment. Keeping attention focused on the task at hand can prove very difficult, impairing work performance or productivity. Even more important, if worry distracts you when you're with friends and loved ones, you can't fully engage them in the moment. Not surprisingly, the quality of intimate relationships can suffer. These are only some of the ways worry can dampen your overall quality of life and get in the way of having fun, feeling joy, and achieving a sense of peace and contentment.

AWARENESS EXERCISE 3:
Impact of Worry

What impact is worry having on your life?

1. Ask yourself how the quality of your relationships or your work is affected by your worry.

2. Have you noticed any effects of worry on your psychological well-being, such as restlessness, losing sleep, or feeling down?

Keep your answers to these questions in mind as you read the next section.

IS WORRY A PROBLEM FOR YOU?

Only you can determine if worry is a problem for you. Perhaps you've been reading this chapter and finding the information about chronic worriers all too familiar. Is the emotional intensity of your worry often out of proportion with the issue at hand? If you take an honest look at yourself and suspect that you would be better off if you worried less, then this book might be helpful to you.

Ask yourself these questions:

- Do you worry about minor things, such as being late, housework, or small repairs to your home or your car?

- Does your worry often contain themes of failure, personal ineffectiveness, or inadequacy?

- When you worry, are other anxiety symptoms present, such as an upset stomach, muscle tension, irritability, or trouble sleeping?

- Does your worry often lead to procrastination?

- Does worry interfere with your concentration when you need to focus on the present moment?

- Does worry keep you from being yourself with others?

If you've answered yes to any of these questions, you might be suffering from chronic worry.

Worry questionnaires provide another way to figure out if you worry too much. Below are some items from the Penn State Worry Questionnaire, a popular worry questionnaire in psychological research.[*] After reading each sentence, ask yourself if it sounds typical of you:

- My worries overwhelm me.

- Many situations make me worry.

---

[*] Reprinted from *Behaviour Research and Therapy*, vol. 28, Meyer et al., Development and validation of the Penn State Worry Questionnaire, pp. 487-495, copyright 1990, with permission from Elsevier.

- I know I should not worry about things, but I just cannot help it.

- When I am under pressure, I worry a lot.

- I am always worrying about something.

- I notice that I have been worrying about things.

- Once I start worrying, I cannot stop.

- I worry all the time.

If most of these sound typical of you, then you might be a chronic worrier. You may also have a problem with worry if just one or two of these are especially true for you. If you're still uncertain whether or not your worry is a problem, go ahead and continue reading. You might find it helpful to practice the strategies in part 2 anyway to see if they improve your quality of life.

HOW TO USE THIS BOOK

The good news is you're not destined to be a worrier forever. Whatever the reasons your worry patterns developed, they can be changed with enough practice of new responses. The next chapter will provide insight into your own personal worry-promoting habits. Part 2 will teach you specific skills with exercises to practice. Once you get the hang of these, part 3 will guide you to apply them in specific areas of your life. You might decide to read the entire book through before trying the exercises. This might make your initial practice a bit easier. Keep in mind that certain strategies might be more useful for you than others. Instead of guessing which ones are best for you beforehand, practice each skill as faithfully as you can and decide which ones work best afterward.

As with all self-help skills, these will only work with dedication and repeated practice. And your attitude is just as important. If you approach this self-help program believing it won't really help you, chances are it won't. People with this approach often practice at first anyway. But at the first sign of difficulty, their experience becomes evidence that they were right to doubt the program in the first place. They don't realize that these skills take a lot of practice before becoming useful. The opposite extreme can also be a problem. Believing that these skills will magically cure all anxiety, discomfort, or emotional pain will soon lead to disappointment. Instead of these extremes, try to approach your practice with an open mind and a sense of curiosity and hope for self-discovery. You can't know for sure whether these skills will be helpful to you, but at least you can give them your best shot and see what happens.

No self-help book can fully substitute for good psychotherapy or counseling. If you suspect that your problems are severe or if you'd like assistance applying the strategies described in this book, use the resources listed in the back to find professional help. If you're already in therapy or counseling, use this book as a resource to share with your therapist. Discuss your experiences with the exercises in your sessions and ask for help understanding the material and how it applies to your own unique situation. Remember, people are not weak for seeking help. On the contrary, this reflects tremendous courage and strength. Any action you take to improve your life shows that you truly care about yourself as well as your loved ones.

CHAPTER 2

Understanding Your Worry and Anxiety

IS ANXIETY NECESSARILY BAD?

As you read in chapter 1, worry is common. Everybody worries once in a while when they're faced with a serious problem and aren't too sure of a solution. Worry itself becomes a problem if you worry constantly or if the worry causes more distress than resolution. But what about anxiety, the feeling you have when your mind perceives possible threat? Is anxiety always a bad thing?

As strange as it may sound, the right amount of anxiety at the right time is very useful. In performance situations, a little anxiety can sharpen your thinking, keeping you alert and on your toes. Imagine how odd an important job interview or a first date would be without the slightest bit of excitement or emotional arousal! Try to think of a time in your own life when the right amount of anxiety was actually helpful. Anxiety only gets in the way when you experience too much of it. Your attention gets distracted by anxious thoughts and feelings, disrupting your self-confidence. It's these secondary effects that prevent you from performing to the best of your ability.

It's important to realize that anxiety itself isn't harmful. Anxiety is a natural reaction when your mind anticipates danger. Because anxiety serves the purpose of alerting you to danger, you might assume something is wrong whenever you feel anxious. Although occasionally you might find yourself in a truly dangerous situation, often the mind is mistaken to perceive danger in the first place. Perhaps the future threat is uncertain or unlikely, or really isn't much of a threat at all. In these instances, you've interpreted your anxiety to mean that real danger lies ahead even though the threat exists only in your mind.

WHAT MAKES UP ANXIETY?

How do you know when you're anxious? Maybe you notice a vague sense of impending doom or you start to feel overwhelmed with discomfort. Anxiety is actually made up of several components or parts that work together to create the overall experience. That's why the first step in understanding your anxiety is to break it down into its individual parts. This allows you to examine each one carefully. The moment you start worrying, a number of ripple effects occur throughout your mind and body. These reactions feed off each other, often quite automatically and out of your awareness. The four main anxiety components are thoughts, subjective feelings, physical sensations, and behavior.

Thoughts

Your thoughts are what you say to yourself inside your head. From time to time worry involves images, or seeing visual pictures in your mind. But worry is usually made up of verbal thoughts, in which you're talking to yourself with words. Everyone has an ongoing dialogue or commentary running through their mind, but they're often completely unaware of it. When thinking is automatic and outside of your awareness, your thoughts are able to influence how you feel. What you say to yourself can leave you feeling happy, proud, depressed, anxious, or a wide range of other emotions. As you become aware of what you're saying to yourself, you'll get the distance you need to put your anxious thoughts into perspective.

When you worry, you're probably asking yourself questions about the future, such as what if something happens or what am I going to do if it happens. Worry can involve predictions or expectations about yourself and your future. For example, you might predict that you wouldn't be able to handle a certain outcome to a situation. Worry can also stem from interpreting past events, such as fearing that a friend is angry with you because she hasn't returned your phone call. Worry is the classic type of anxious thought, and often anxiety begins with worry. However, anxious thoughts can occur in response to anxious feelings, bodily sensations, or behavior. For example, you might notice your heart racing and have the thought that something must be wrong.

Over the next several days, tune into your own inner dialogue. Start to notice the different types of thoughts you have and under what circumstances you have them.

1. What thoughts run through your mind when you're feeling anxious? Although you might already be painfully aware of your worry, look at these thoughts carefully and determine exactly what you are saying to yourself as you worry.

2. How do these thoughts impact other anxiety components, including your feelings, physical sensations, and behavior?

3. Compare the thoughts you have when you're anxious to those you have at other times, such as when you're feeling calm, happy, or angry.

Subjective Feelings

Your feelings are very subjective. They reflect your own unique internal experience of your thoughts, sensations, and behavior. When you experience anxious thoughts and physical sensations of anxiety, you might have feelings of discomfort or impending doom. Feeling irritable or frustrated is also common during worry. Anxious feelings certainly result from anxious thoughts and worries. But if you're already experiencing feelings of anxiety, you are even more prone to anxious thinking patterns than if you were feeling calm and relaxed.

Physical Sensations

Sensations occur in your body during anxiety. These are your physiological responses and reactions. Some people experience intense physical signs of anxiety, while other people hardly notice any bodily sensations. Some physical sensations of anxiety are under our voluntary control, even if we do them unintentionally. One example is muscle tension, such as clenching your jaw, making fists, or furrowing your forehead. Another example involves your breathing, when you take short and shallow breaths. These are the most common bodily sensations during worry.

Other anxiety sensations are not under your direct control. These include your heart racing or pounding, upset stomach, shaking, sweating, flushing, and rising body temperature. These more dramatic anxiety symptoms tend to occur as a specific situation approaches, such as just before you give a speech. But they can also result from intense worry as your thinking makes a specific feared event seem closer and closer in your mind.

AWARENESS EXERCISE 5:
Notice Anxious Feelings and Sensations

Identify the feelings and bodily sensations you experience during anxiety and worry:

1. Which physical sensations do you notice when you worry?

2. Do you get the same feelings every time, or does it depend on the situation?

3. Do your feelings and sensations change or grow as your worry continues?

4. Be on the lookout for when your muscles tense up. Which muscles carry around extra tension most often?

5. How is your breathing different when you're calm and relaxed compared to when you're anxious?

6. When do you experience more dramatic sensations, such as your heart racing or feeling flushed?

Behavior

The behavior component of worry is what you do when you're anxious. Any action you take, or don't take, makes up your anxious behavior. The main behavior associated with anxiety and worry is avoidance or withdrawal. Anxiety involves your perception that something unwanted and threatening could happen. So the natural behavioral response is to get away from the threat or withdraw from the problematic situation, as well as to avoid similar situations in the future.

Chronic worriers often have a difficult time figuring out exactly what situations they avoid. This is because worry can span across many different situations and places. If you're a worrier, you might avoid social situations, such as attending social events where you'll meet new people, confronting someone, saying no or asserting yourself in other ways, speaking your mind, or looking people in the eye. You may also avoid certain places related to your worry; for example, not driving down a particular street because you worry about car accidents. Other avoidance behaviors include turning down a promotion or project at work or not even applying for that dream job due to a fear of failing.

Outwardly avoiding certain places and situations is the most obvious form of avoidance behavior. But worriers often have very subtle avoidance behaviors too. Common examples include seeking reassurance from other people about your worries, checking the things you worry about to make sure everything is okay, and mentally distracting yourself from your worry instead of thinking it all the way through. Chronic worriers might change the radio or television channel every time the news comes on to avoid hearing about tragic events. Are you a perfectionist? If so, you might double- or triple-check yourself even when it's not important or you don't need to be accurate. Those who worry about being on time will leave for an appointment extremely early just to avoid being late. People who worry about being productive enough at work often take on more work projects than they can handle at any one time. A woman who worries about her husband's safety might call him repeatedly throughout the day to check on him. Behaviors like this last one can come across as overbearing and annoying, unintentionally pushing loved ones away. These behaviors are considered avoidant because, although you do them to feel safe, ultimately they keep you from facing the fears underneath your worry.

Worry can also prevent you from taking any action at all, becoming quite paralyzing. This behavior is a bit like a deer freezing in your headlights on a country road. But in the case of your worry, no action is taken because the threat is too vague or it lies too far in the future. Maybe you avoid taking action out of fear that the result won't be effective or good enough. Procrastination is very common among women who worry. Yet the simple act of putting something off makes the task even more anxiety provoking. Instead of feeling empowered by accomplishing what you set out to do, your confidence fades.

All of these anxiety behaviors have something important in common: you engage in them when you're feeling overwhelmed for temporary relief. But this relief comes at a very high price. Avoidance behaviors reinforce your anxious thoughts, making them seem stronger and more credible. Any hidden beliefs that those situations really are threatening and you won't be able to handle them are strengthened. Instead of learning that the things you worry about can be faced head-on and managed, your anxiety about them only grows. Plus, you never get to see what would have happened if you had faced a particular situation, so you deprive yourself of the chance to see how things would have turned out and how you would have coped. This is how avoidance can leave you feeling powerless and out of control.

AWARENESS EXERCISE 6:
Notice Anxious Behavior

Think back over the times you've felt worried and anxious.

1. What situations have you avoided because of your worry?

2. If complete avoidance of a situation wasn't possible, were there still certain actions you didn't take? For example, a woman worried about looking foolish at a party might go to the party but avoid striking up any conversations.

3. In your close or intimate relationships, do you sometimes avoid expressing how you really feel, asserting your needs, or having a heart-to-heart talk when something's bothering you?

4. In addition to avoiding certain situations and actions, which subtle avoidance behaviors do you do when you're worried?

- Do you seek out reassurance from other people to feel better?

- Do you check certain objects in response to a worry?

- Do you call your loved ones repeatedly to make sure they're safe?

WORRY SPIRALS: REACTIONS TO REACTIONS

These four anxiety components—thoughts, feelings, sensations, and behavior—don't exist in isolation, with each one independently growing on its own. Instead, each anxious thought, feeling, sensation, and behavior is an immediate reaction to the previous event. Anxiety often seems to come on suddenly or unexpectedly. You may not notice it building until it reaches a very high level. But your anxiety is actually a process. It's made up of a series of thoughts, feelings, sensations, and behaviors. Each component is an immediate and automatic reaction to the previous one, allowing your anxiety to quickly build upon itself. In other words, anxiety involves a spiral of interactions between your thoughts, feelings, sensations, and behavior, any one of which can get the ball rolling.

Have you ever found yourself swept up with anxiety and worry not knowing where it came from? Take this example of Julia, a twenty-eight-year-old legal assistant working in a large law firm in New York. Her worry spirals often began with worry about an upcoming meeting at work (thought). Next she'd notice her hands getting clammy, her breath feeling short, and her muscles getting tense (physical sensations). Soon she'd find herself feeling distressed and apprehensive (subjective feelings). She would then tell herself that something really must be wrong and worry about all the possible negative outcomes that could result from the meeting (more thoughts). Often she wound up skipping the meetings altogether (behavior), spending the rest of the day worrying about the fact that she worries too much (even more thoughts).

This anxiety process can begin with any of its four components. But for chronic worriers, the process often begins with worried thoughts. The worry could be triggered by a reminder from your immediate surroundings. Or it might suddenly pop into your mind unprovoked. In either case, the moment you begin to worry, a vicious cycle is set in motion, with each reaction giving rise to the next. One simple thought quickly spirals into a cyclone of anxious feelings, sensations, behavior, and more thoughts. These worry spirals happen very quickly, long before you realize what's going on. Instead of noticing each individual event, you're only aware of your general discomfort. That's because these sequences of reactions have become very automatic, much like the sequence of specific actions and movements involved in driving your car. Your own individual worry spirals have occurred so many times before that they've developed into habits no longer in your awareness. Each time a worry spiral unfolds, that particular sequence of thoughts, feelings, sensations, and behavior gets stored in your memory and becomes a stronger habit.

RECOGNIZE YOUR OWN WORRY SPIRALS

You've already identified the separate components of your worry spirals in the previous exercises. But it can be difficult to figure out how each one interacts with the others during times of high anxiety. The next step in understanding your worry and anxiety is to discover your own personal patterns of thoughts, feelings, sensations, and behavior.

One way to start is to go back over the individual components you've already identified. How do you see certain anxious thoughts connected to certain feelings, sensations, and behavior? How do certain feelings and sensations lead to other thoughts and behavior? How do your anxiety behaviors make you feel and think afterward? Once you start tying these together, you begin to see how your own individual moment-to-moment reactions keep your anxiety building.

Another approach is to be on the lookout when you worry in the future. The next time you notice yourself worrying, try to be very curious about how you got there. What thoughts, feelings, and sensations have you just experienced? See if you can trace the sequence back to the beginning. When did you last feel calm or not anxious? Then what happened? Did your sequence begin with a worried thought this time? Was it in response to something that just happened? Did you hear or see something that reminded you of your worry, or did the worry just appear in your mind for no clear reason? Once you began to worry, what feelings and sensations followed? What did you say to yourself in response to them? Did you change your behavior in any way during this sequence, such as checking something, seeking reassurance, or avoiding doing something? If so, what thoughts, feelings, and sensations followed? Asking these questions can help uncover the sequences of events that make up your own worry spirals.

AWARENESS EXERCISE 7:
Retrace Your Worry Spirals

Select a recent experience with worry and anxiety that you still remember well.

1. Take a few moments, closing your eyes if it helps, and imagine yourself back in that situation.

- What were the circumstances surrounding the situation? Begin with the last thing you remember.

- How did you feel emotionally?

- What sensations did you notice in your body?

- What thoughts were running through your mind?

- What behaviors were you doing?

2. As you begin to identify each individual reaction, work your way backward in time, seeing if you can remember what was happening in your body and mind the moment before. Trace your sequence of reactions all the way back to the beginning, when you weren't feeling anxious at all. What seemed to trigger this spiral in the first place? As you identify your specific worry spiral for that example, write down the sequence on a piece of paper.

3. Come back to this exercise later and do the same thing with a different worry episode. Use a new sheet of paper to record the sequence of thoughts, feelings, sensations, and behaviors.

4. Compare the two examples. Can you find any similarities or patterns in your reactions? Do the same thoughts appear in both? You might want to work through several examples to discover certain patterns or spirals. How do you usually respond to early cues of worry and anxiety that encourage your spirals to develop?

The effort you put into this exercise now will pay off as you practice the strategies presented in the rest of this book. The more aware you become of your worry spirals, the better you'll be able to change their course and try some new responses in their place.

PART II

HOW TO OVERCOME YOUR WORRY: SPECIFIC STRATEGIES

CHAPTER 3

Track Worry Cues and Triggers

WHY MONITORING IS SO IMPORTANT

Hopefully you've had the chance to start tuning into the thoughts, feelings, sensations, and behavior that make up your own worry spirals. Or maybe you tried some of the awareness exercises but found them nothing but frustrating! Starting to monitor your worry and anxiety can be tough because you've probably tried everything you can not to think of your worries. When worry already feels like a miserable energy-zapping waste of time, tracking it and devoting even more attention to it can seem pretty absurd. But ask yourself honestly how well your strategy of just trying not to think about it has worked. You may have even noticed that the harder you try *not* to think of a worry, the more your mind wants to return to it.

We human beings are not very good at suppressing our thoughts, or purposefully trying not to think of something. Plenty of research shows that these efforts often backfire, causing a flood of the unwanted thoughts the instant you let your guard down (Wegner 1989). When you put mental energy into trying not to worry, you create a paradox for your mind. It actually has to hold onto the worrisome thought to scan all the activity going through your head and screen out the worry. Plus, you send a message that some thoughts are dangerous and shouldn't be examined. It's time to try the opposite approach: actively watching for worry cues, looking at worries in a new, objective way, and reacting to worrisome thoughts, feelings, and sensations with conscious choice and a sense of purpose.

Monitoring your worry spirals is a must because you first need to become aware of all the automatic reactions and response habits you've built up over the years. It's so easy to get swept up into worry the moment it starts. You soon feel helpless, as if you're a victim of your own mind. Monitoring is the first step in reversing this process because you start to take charge of your reactions. This sends the message that you can face your fears and problems head-on and no longer need to hide from them.

Tracking your worry spirals is much easier said than done. Many women struggle with this first step because it can be difficult to pick up on small shifts in anxiety when you're already feeling anxious and worried most of the time. Don't be discouraged if you discover that this takes a lot of patience and practice. Try the exercises described in the next section to self-monitor your worry on a regular basis. You'll learn how to build in reminders to check in with yourself frequently as you begin to develop new habits.

HOW TO TRACK THE WORRY PROCESS OBJECTIVELY

Before you begin the monitoring exercises, keep in mind two key points that are crucial for doing them effectively. First, all self-monitoring must be done on the spot, capturing the very moment you are experiencing. It's tempting to go back in time and try to remember how you were feeling yesterday or last week. But our retrospective memories often become distorted by time as well as by our emotions, so they aren't always reliable. To really understand your worry spirals, look at each specific instance as soon as you catch it. On-the-spot monitoring will get you ready to apply the coping strategies described in the next chapters at the exact time they'll be most useful.

Second, watch for your worry cues and your moment-to-moment reactions objectively. Instead of subjectively getting caught up with your anxiety and worry, try to become an objective observer of every thought, feeling, sensation, and behavior as if you're noticing it for the first time. No matter what's happening inside you at the moment, examine your experience as if you're a scientist who is curious about how something works. Instead of judging your anxiety and worry as bad or getting down on yourself for having them, take a step back and give yourself a bit of distance. The goal of self-monitoring is to uncover your own sequence of reactions to things that occur both inside of you and in the outside world. The way to accomplish this is to describe what is actually happening as concretely as you can, just as a chemist would describe how chemicals are reacting to one another during a laboratory experiment.

MONITORING EXERCISE 1:
Rate Your Anxiety

1. Find a notepad and pencil or pen. Draw a horizontal line across the first page and write the number 0 on the left end and 100 on the right end. Put a hash mark in the middle and write the number 50 below it. It will look something like this:

You'll use this simple scale to monitor your anxiety levels throughout this self-help program. Now try it for the first time. Ask yourself this question: If 100 is as anxious as I can possibly imagine, and 0 is completely and absolutely relaxed, how am I feeling right now? Of course there is no single "correct" answer to this question, but write down the number that best represents your current anxiety level. Put an exact number on your anxiety in the same sort of way your thermostat generates a number to indicate the current room temperature. This is the first step in looking at your anxiety and worry objectively.

2. Once you have come up with a number between 0 and 100 and written it down, ask yourself how you came up with it. Try to identify all you tuned into to arrive at that particular number. Underneath your anxiety rating, write down any thoughts you noticed. On the next line, list your subjective feelings. Then on the line underneath, jot down all bodily sensations. Finally, list any behaviors or movements you did or felt the urge to do. Be sure to list everything you notice that makes up your current experience. Here are some questions to ask:

- What were you just saying to yourself the split second before you came up with that rating?

- Were you having doubtful thoughts about whether this book can help you or whether you'll able to use it successfully?

- What subjective feelings did you notice? For example, were you feeling helpless, hopeless, frustrated, hopeful, or excited?

- Are certain muscles tense or relaxed?

- Are you sitting or breathing a certain way?

- Are you fidgeting or making any other anxiety-related movements?

Don't force yourself to decide what to include here—just write down everything you notice about your experience as matter-of-factly as you can.

3. Use the rest of your notepad as a diary to monitor your anxiety level several times a day, *every day*. Each page of your notebook can represent a different day. Each entry should begin with the time of day and a short description of what's happening around you, such as "sitting at my desk at work" or "just hung up the phone after talking to Mary." Then record a number between 0 and 100 to reflect your current anxiety rating and a description of whatever thoughts, feelings, sensations, and behaviors you noticed came up with that rating, exactly as you have just done in the previous steps. Remember to take time out throughout your day to make your diary entries—don't go back and write your entries after-the-fact from memory. Don't be tempted to skip the step of writing this down! Putting your entries in writing is part of what makes your monitoring objective. Plus, you'll be able to go back through your diary to track your progress, look for patterns, and learn what seems to trigger your worry. If you want even more practice to maximize your efforts, you can mentally monitor your anxiety by just thinking of a current rating. Do this in addition to the four to five times a day you make a written diary entry.

Set a Schedule for Monitoring

The trick to successful monitoring is finding a way to remind yourself to do it throughout the day. One strategy is to decide ahead of time when you will do this as part of your daily routine. You might decide to make your first diary entry of the day when you get out of bed, your second entry when you take your lunch break, your third entry as soon as you get home from work, and your fourth entry after you eat dinner. Every hour on the hour works well for some people if they wear a watch regularly. Another strategy is to pick something that happens frequently during your day as a reminder to check in and rate your anxiety; for example, each time you switch tasks at work, leave home for the next errand, or stop at a red light while driving. These are all momentary events that can remind you to step back, rate your anxiety, and take an objective inventory of your thoughts, feelings, sensations, and behavior. Even letting the phone ring an extra time before picking up can give you a second to check in. Obviously, some of these (such as when you're driving!) aren't times when you can make one of your written diary entries. But the idea is to start the habit of monitoring as often as you can throughout the day with at least four written diary entries per day.

On the next page is a diary entry from Linda, a chronic worrier with a lot of stress at work. Linda has chosen to make one of her daily written entries at 9:45 A.M. each day when she takes her midmorning break.

Tuesday, Nov. 5th

9:45 a.m.

Sitting at my desk. My supervisor just asked for the project I'm still working on.

Anxiety rating: 40

Thoughts: How am I going to get this done before lunch? Why is my supervisor always so short with me? I hate this job.

Subjective feelings: Frustrated and cranky—also still feeling sad from that dream last night.

Physical sensations: My shoulders are tense and sore, butterflies and knots in my stomach, tightness in my upper chest.

Behaviors: Biting my fingernails, tapping my pencil against my desk, feeling the urge to hide out in the bathroom for a few minutes.

CATCH YOUR WORRY SPIRALS EARLIER AND EARLIER

Now that you've started to monitor your anxiety levels and become aware of what components make up your experience, the next step is to trace each instance back further and further. In some cases, you might even discover where the worry spiral began by identifying the original trigger that got it going in the first place. Worry spirals are much like a snowball rolling down a mountain: they gain momentum and grow at increasingly fast rates over a short period of time. Therefore, the earlier you catch a worry spiral developing, the weaker it will be. Switching gears by trying out a new coping response will be easier to do. You'll also increase the chances that your coping response will effectively interrupt the worry process. Use this next monitoring exercise to help you look for earlier and earlier signs that you're in the midst of a worry spiral. Retracing the specific sequence of events can help you discover what might have triggered that particular worry spiral.

MONITORING EXERCISE 2:
Examine Anxiety Episodes

1. Over the next week or so, be on the lookout for a time when you make a diary entry with an anxiety rating of 50 or higher. This reveals that you're feeling at least a moderate amount of anxiety. At that time, go ahead and record the situation happening around you as well as any thoughts, feelings, sensations, and behaviors that are contributing to the overall experience.

2. Once you've finished your entry in the usual way, take out a separate piece of paper and turn it

horizontally so that the page is longer left to right than it is top to bottom. Near the right edge of the paper, write down the very last thought, feeling, sensation, or behavior that occurred as you made your anxiety rating. If you noticed a couple of these simultaneously, go ahead and jot down more than one thing.

3. Now put a small arrow pointing to the right just to the left of your answer. Ask yourself, What was happening the moment before this? Perhaps a particular thought ran through your mind that served as a cue for certain muscles to tense up or for your jaw to clench. Write down your answer to this question to the left of the arrow. You can probably already see where this exercise is going. Put another arrow pointing to the right just to the left of your last answer and again ask yourself, What was happening the moment before this? Keep tracing your worry spiral back in this way as far as you can. You might even discover that you were feeling calm and relaxed until someone said something to you or gave you a certain look. Or maybe it all started when an image of something terrible popped into your mind. Try to add this exercise to the regular daily monitoring described in the previous exercise once a day or at least every time when your anxiety levels goes above 50.

Let's say that in the diary entry above, Linda had rated her anxiety at 50 instead of 40. Here's how this second exercise might look:

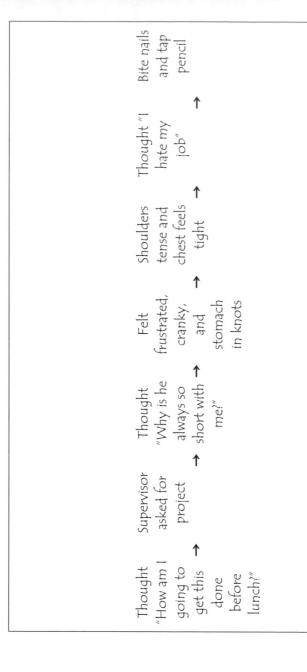

Thought "How am I going to get this done before lunch?" → Supervisor asked for project → Thought "Why is he always so short with me?" → Felt frustrated, cranky, and stomach in knots → Shoulders tense and chest feels tight → Thought "I hate my job" → Bite nails and tap pencil

BREAKING OLD HABITS

Once you start these monitoring exercises, you're on the way to breaking your old habits of reacting to worry cues and triggers in anxiety-provoking ways. You may have already noticed that roughly the same sequence of reactions happens time after time across worry spirals. These reactions have been practiced many times, so they've been built up in your memory. Strong habits of reactions are hard to break because they're so easy to activate. That's why they feel so automatic and get going without any effort at all.

On the other hand, trying to do something new takes a lot of effort and certainly doesn't feel automatic. This is why the coping strategy exercises described in the next few chapters will probably be very difficult at the beginning. The good news is that with practice they will become easier and easier to apply. With each practice attempt, you'll be building up new response sequences to store in your memory. In other words, new coping responses will become new habits. Not only will your old habits of responding get weaker from not getting to run their course, but your new coping response habits will get triggered more readily. Worry cues and triggers will start to take on a new meaning. When you notice a worry running through your mind, tense shoulder muscles, or a nervous stomach, these cues will no longer have to mean that you're in for a miserable ride. Instead, they begin to look like opportunities, letting you know that you have the perfect chance to practice one of your new coping strategies.

BUILDING NEW HABITS: FOUR BASIC STRATEGIES

You can't break old habits of reactions by simply not doing them anymore. You also need to find something new and different to do instead. So what are these new coping responses that you can practice? Each of the next four chapters will teach you a coping strategy that targets at least one of the four different components of anxiety. Learning all of these strategies is best because you'll develop several skills to use whenever you catch a worry spiral. You might find that the strategy for gaining a new perspective works best in some situations while the strategy of relaxing your body and mind works best in others. Practice each strategy faithfully for at least a week or two before deciding which ones work best for you. Each strategy will take a lot of practice before you become skilled at it, so don't be surprised if they feel strange and don't have an impact immediately. With a little persistence and practice, most people are pleasantly surprised by how soon they start to turn their worry spirals around.

Put Your Worries in Perspective

The first strategy targets anxious thoughts and worries by putting them into perspective. In chapter 4, you'll learn how to treat your thoughts as guesses, interpretations, and predictions rather than facts that must be true. This allows you to examine them and look at a single situation in several different ways. You'll see that there are many different ways to view yourself and the world around you and that you can exercise choice in how you respond to your thoughts.

Face the Things You Fear

The second strategy targets the tendency to avoid the things you fear. In chapter 5, you'll learn how to face people, situations, and emotions that are linked to your worries. When people worry, they're usually thinking about the things they fear, but their mind spins around the issue as if they need protection from confronting it head-on. They wind up feeling more and more anxious, helpless, and hopeless, with that awful sense of impending doom. But these feelings are secondary, cued by other reactions in the worry spiral. The underlying emotions that make us most human often get lost in this process. Chapter 5 will help you identify even the most subtle things you might be avoiding and teach you how to confront them in a manageable, step-by-step way. You'll learn that you can approach any situation you choose without giving in to that urge to avoid and escape. You'll see that you can handle any emotions that might come up in the process, no matter how vulnerable you feel.

Relax Yourself

The strategies described in chapter 6 target the bodily sensations of anxiety with physical relaxation techniques. Although most of these techniques are believed to work by changing your physiology directly, the body and mind are never really separate. Calming your mind and creating a subjective sense of peace and relaxation are also goals of chapter 6.

Stay in the Present

The final strategy, in chapter 7, targets the mind's tendency to wander off into the future or back to the past at the expense of the present. Instead of reacting to illusions that haven't happened yet or to interpretations of the past, you can live in the present moment and fully experience all that life has to offer as it unfolds. You'll learn how to bring your mind back to the present moment when it has wandered.

You'll practice observing yourself and your surroundings in an accepting, compassionate, and nonjudgmental way, free from expectations.

EVIDENCE FOR THIS APPROACH TO WORRY

All of the strategies described in this book have been tested in psychological research. Many women suffering from chronic worry and diagnosed with generalized anxiety disorder participated in these research studies. During this research, both women and men learned some combination of worry coping strategies from a therapist. With enough practice, many people enjoyed significant and lasting improvements in their lives (Borkovec and Ruscio 2001; Gould et al. 2004).

Most of these research studies included a type of therapy called *cognitive behavioral therapy*. One part of this therapy includes *cognitive therapy* or *cognitive restructuring*, which involves putting your thoughts in perspective, something you'll learn about in chapter 4. Another part of cognitive behavioral therapy involves exposure to worry-related situations, as you'll do in the exercises in chapter 5. The relaxation techniques described in chapter 6 are also commonly found in cognitive behavioral therapy. The cognitive behavioral approach chosen for this book was based largely on the therapy of Tom Borkovec and his colleagues at Pennsylvania State University (Borkovec et al. 2002). They've been researching this therapy for worriers over the past twenty years. Some of the cognitive behavioral techniques described in this book are also informed by the work of David Barlow, Michelle Craske, and their colleagues (Zinbarg, Craske, and Barlow 1993; Brown, O'Leary, and Barlow 2001). If you're interested in learning more about cognitive behavioral therapy research, you can read about each individual study in research review articles (Borkovec and Ruscio 2001; Gould et al. 2004).

Finally, the approach of focusing on the present moment described in chapter 7 is also part of the Penn State cognitive behavioral therapy program described above. Newer therapies for worry have expanded on this idea by teaching *mindfulness* strategies, in which people practice attending to the present moment in very structured and intentional ways (Orsillo, Roemer, and Barlow 2003). In addition, one therapy research study suggests that mindfulness practice alone might be helpful to worriers who suffer from generalized anxiety disorder (Kabat-Zinn et al. 1992).

CHAPTER 4

Gain a New Perspective

YOUR THOUGHTS AREN'T FACTS

Our worries are filled with hidden predictions, expectations, and assumptions about ourselves, other people, and our future. Once a worry enters our mind, we instantly want to prepare for the worst. So we react as if what we fear is guaranteed to happen. Our minds and bodies shift into high gear, and the sequence of reactions that makes up our worry spirals starts to snowball. But worrying in our usual way actually prevents us from seeing ourselves and our fears clearly. We're so busy reacting that we aren't able to look at our thoughts in new ways and truly think them all the way through. Instead, we wind up convinced that disaster lies ahead, so we keep on worrying in an attempt to prepare for it.

The goal of this chapter is to help you examine your worries objectively. This is very different from simply substituting "happy" thoughts for anxious thoughts. Life is not always a rose garden, and tragic events do happen. In fact, none of us will get through life without some degree of heartache, pain, and suffering. But for too many women, worry causes a completely different kind of suffering that is truly unnecessary. When you're always expecting the worst and assuming you won't be able to handle it, you ignore a lot of important information about yourself and the world around you. The exercises in this chapter will help you see your worries in all their different shades of gray rather than as just black and white.

Worry as a False Sense of Certainty

When we're in the middle of a worry spiral, we don't realize that most situations are open to interpretation. Most of the things we worry about are at least somewhat ambiguous, and the future is always unknown because it hasn't happened yet. Sometimes this uncertainty is exciting. Imagine how dull life would be if everything was 100 percent predictable. But sometimes this uncertainty feels unsettling. We long for that magic crystal ball to tell us how things will turn out so at least we can know for sure.

Many people rely on worry to cope with life's uncertainties. Although worry feels awful and leads you into a vicious cycle, worry also makes things seem more certain than they actually are. But the brief sense of comfort you get from feeling more certain comes at too high a price. When you worry, you fill in the blanks with interpretations and predictions of threat. You might feel more prepared for the worst and more certain about your situation, but you also become anxious, miserable, and insecure in the process. Plus, the more people worry, the more they see uncertainty as a problem (Dugas, Freeston, and Ladouceur 1997). This chapter will help you put your worries in perspective by exploring the uncertainty and ambiguity that always surrounds you. Instead of creating only one scenario to feel more certain, you can consider all possibilities and learn to see things from many different viewpoints.

Treat Your Thoughts as Guesses

As you practice each of the steps described in the next section, always start by reminding yourself that each thought is only a guess about the meaning of an event or about what could happen in the future. We all try to make sense of what's going on around us by explaining to ourselves what has just happened or what will soon happen. But worries often are just predictions about the future. They're your best guess about what will happen, how others will respond, and how you'll cope. These thoughts are as automatic as a reflex. You think them so naturally and easily that they're out of your awareness unless you purposefully tune into them. Until you become aware of your thoughts and treat them as guesses instead of facts, your mind and body will react to them as if they're true. Instead you can take a step back to question them and compare them to other ways of looking at your situation.

Sara: Reading into the Situation

Let's take an example from the life of Sara, a thirty-year-old newspaper editor living in Chicago who invited a new friend from work out to dinner. They agreed to meet at the restaurant, but when Sara arrived her friend wasn't there. She went ahead and got a table, letting the hostess know that she was expecting a friend. Ten minutes passed and her friend had not appeared. Sara went ahead and ordered a drink, wondering why her friend was late and if she would be coming at all. *Perhaps this is just some kind of mistake*, Sara thought. *Or maybe she couldn't find parking, she's caught in traffic, or her boss made her stay late at work.*

Twenty minutes later, Sara called her friend's cell phone number. But there was no answer and the call went straight to voice mail. Sara realized that her own cell phone had been turned off, but there were no voice mail messages. Sara now dismissed all the simple explanations that had gone through her mind before. Certainly her friend would have called if any of these were the case. So Sara did what many people would: she started reading into the situation, coming up with her own interpretation to explain why her friend wasn't there. Her friend must have decided not to come and didn't bother to cancel, probably because she was only pretending to like Sara at work. Sara's interpretation of this incident left her feeling dejected, insecure, and humiliated. After waiting fifty minutes without her cell phone ringing, Sara finally decided to pay the check and leave. Convinced that her so-called friend stood her up, Sara spent the rest of the evening and most of the next day worrying about it: *Why doesn't she like me? What if I keep trying to meet people only to get rejected? What if my date this Saturday stands me up too? I wouldn't be able to handle that . . .*

Later the following afternoon, Sara checked her voice mail again after a meeting. There was a voice mail message from her friend, recorded less than one minute before Sara turned on her phone at the restaurant. As it turned out, her friend had called to say that her son was sick and she wouldn't be able to meet Sara after all. But Sara's cell phone carrier takes approximately two minutes to make a voice mail message available. She had missed her friend's call to cancel without even realizing it! The point of Sara's story is that there are many different ways to interpret any event. Even more important, how you interpret a situation leads you to feel a certain way about it.

PUT YOUR THOUGHTS IN PERSPECTIVE

This next section walks you through five specific steps to apply each time you catch yourself worrying. You'll start by taking your worry through each step in writing. The best way to do this is to get a notebook or a journal to track your worries and to work each worrisome thought through these steps. As you get better and better at putting your thoughts in perspective, you'll find yourself following these steps automatically on your own. But at first, keep a running list of your main worries as you discover them throughout the day by means of the regular monitoring you learned in chapter 3. Each day, you'll take at least fifteen to twenty minutes and walk each worry through these specific steps in writing. You'll use this same format to work through the specific worry topics in part 3. The rest of this section is designed to teach you each of the five steps:

Step 1: Get specific. Identify exactly what you're saying to yourself.

Step 2: Generate alternatives. Brainstorm other outcomes and interpretations.

Step 3: Look at the evidence. Examine the likelihood of each possibility.

Step 4: Suppose the worst did happen. Follow your worry to conclusion.

Step 5: Explore new perspectives. Summarize to create a more balanced perspective.

Step 1: Get Specific

The first step is to identify exactly what you are saying to yourself when you worry. Once you notice that your thoughts are creating anxiety, focus in on a specific instance or situation captured by that worry. Get as detailed and concrete as you can about *what* you're worried will happen. It takes a lot of practice to narrow a vague and general worry down to a concrete prediction or interpretation that is so specific you can later say for sure whether or not it actually happened.

PERSPECTIVE EXERCISE 1:
Get Specific

1. Pick a worry you've discovered today during your daily monitoring. Write this worry topic at the top of a new page in your journal. If you haven't yet started your regular daily monitoring, see the exercises in chapter 3 for specific instructions.

2. Underneath this general worry topic, write down a specific instance, event, or situation that best represents your recent worry. Get as detailed as you can.

3. Figure out if this worry is about the past or the future. Write down the following information:

   • Past event: If you're worrying about a situation that has already happened, how are you interpreting it or explaining it to yourself? What are you telling yourself about it that leaves you feeling anxious?

- Future event: If your worry is about an upcoming situation or about something that could happen in the future, figure out exactly what you're predicting will happen or exactly what you fear could happen. This should be so specific that another person could objectively see whether or not this event has occurred at a later point in time.

4. Now try to get your anxious thought as specific as you possibly can. Be on the lookout for these obstacles to getting specific:

- General terms: Watch out for general terms that have subjective meaning to you but cannot be verified objectively. For example, if you're worried about a particular situation coming up in the future because you'll be a "failure," push yourself to clarify what you mean. What exactly are you predicting will happen when you use that word? Once that event has occurred, how will you be able to go back and determine whether or not the outcome you predicted has happened?

- Unlimited time frame: Another trouble spot comes up when worries have a never-ending time frame. If this is the case for your current anxious thought, force yourself to find a point in the future that reflects when you think your prediction could happen or will have happened.

5. Once you have narrowed down what you are specifically worried about, summarize it in a sentence. Now make a column on the left side of the page, label it "Get Specific," and enter your sentence in this column under the Get Specific heading.

Stacy: Worried about School, Her Career, and an Aimless Future

Let's work through this exercise for Stacy, a nineteen-year-old single college student who often finds herself burdened by vague worries about school and her future career.

1. During her daily monitoring, Stacy discovered that she worries a lot about school. She puts this topic at the top of a page in her journal.

2. As she searches for a specific instance, event, or situation that best represents her worries about school, Stacy realizes that she often finds herself sitting in class wondering if she will actually finish college and earn her bachelor's degree. She decides to write down "I'm worried about finishing school and earning my degree" underneath the general worry topic of "school."

3. Stacy easily sees that this particular worry is about something happening in the future. She asks herself exactly what she fears could happen, and writes down the following prediction: "I'll never finish school."

4. Now Stacy really challenges herself to get even more specific. She looks for general terms in the sentence she's just written and wonders about her use of the word "never." As she reads on, Stacy discovers that her prediction has an unlimited time frame. She asks herself, How far into the future is reasonable to expect I'll either finish school or decide not to continue? Stacy tries to get her anxious thought of "I'll never finish school" into a very specific prediction by getting clear about the timing of the outcome. A couple of possibilities come to mind: "I won't have my degree four years from now" and "I'll need six years instead of four years to graduate." Notice that in Stacy's earlier version ("I'll never finish school"), another person would have to wait for Stacy's life to end to know whether or not her prediction came true. But after doing step 4, Stacy herself could look back after either four years or six years and see if her prediction came true.

5. Now that Stacy has narrowed down a particular worry about school, she discovers that what really bothers her is the possibility that four years from now she won't graduate college with her peers. She writes the following specific prediction in the Get Specific column: "I will not have my degree four years from now."

Step 2: Generate Alternatives

Now that you've gotten specific, the second step is to generate alternatives. Once you have a specific prediction, assumption, or interpretation to examine, you can start coming up with alternative ones. The goal of this step is to list as many alternatives as possible. Brainstorm by pushing yourself to think of many different possibilities, however unlikely and silly they might seem. Now is not the time to judge them or to dismiss the ones that appear unlikely. You'll evaluate them later. The goal of this exercise is to free up your thinking, making your mind as flexible as you can. Generating many different possibilities keeps you from getting stuck on the worst possible outcome or the original perspective that automatically came to you while worrying.

PERSPECTIVE EXERCISE 2:
Generate Alternatives

1. On the same piece of paper, make another column just to the right of your Get Specific column and label it "Alternatives."

2. In this column, list as many alternatives to the specific thought you've identified as you can. Make sure you come up with a full spectrum of outcomes or interpretations, ranging from the best possible one to the worst.

- If you're worrying about something happening in the future, what are some alternative ways it could turn out?

- If you're worrying about an event that has already happened, what are some other interpretations or ways of looking at your situation that another person might see?

Stacy might generate alternatives to her prediction "I will not have my degree four years from now" that include "I'll graduate on time with my class," "I'll take summer school classes and graduate early," and "I won't graduate with my class, but I'll finish my degree the next semester."

3. Once you've made your list of alternatives, go back through each one to see if you can generate even more. There might be one aspect of your situation or prediction that hasn't changed throughout your list. Try to find variations for each of the alternatives you have so far. It might even be worthwhile to share this exercise with a significant other, family member, or friend, who might come up with alternatives you haven't considered.

Stacy discovered that all of her alternatives centered on when she would or wouldn't graduate. She then came up with more, such as "I'll find a job that I love during college and choose not to finish my degree" and "I'll start my own dot-com business instead."

Step 3: Look at the Evidence

The goal of this next step is to go back over each alternative on your list and compare it to your original specific thought. You'll examine the likelihood of your original anxious thought as well as each alternative. You'll also look at the evidence behind each one. It's easy to think of facts and information to support your anxious thought. That's why you'll challenge yourself to look for all the evidence you can find against it too. When people worry, they often make the mistake of interpreting their anxious feelings as evidence that what they're worrying about is pretty likely.

Feeling anxious naturally sets you up to believe that the likelihood of your anxious thought is much higher than it probably actually is. That's why you'll really need to question yourself about your initial likelihood estimates. Just because something feels true or likely to happen doesn't necessarily mean that it is. Can you think of any times when you were 100 percent certain that something you worried about would happen or had happened and later found out that you were wrong? Maybe you were sure you wouldn't get into a certain school, but then you were accepted. Or you were convinced someone was upset with you, only to learn later that they weren't.

PERSPECTIVE EXERCISE 3:
Look at the Evidence

1. Make a column labeled "Evidence" just to the right of your Alternatives column.

2. Taking your original specific anxious thought from the first column, ask yourself, What are the chances this has happened or will happen? On a scale of 0 to 100, come up with a percent likelihood that reflects how realistic or likely this possibility is. Zero percent likelihood means it's impossible, and 100 percent means it's definite and certain. Write your likelihood estimate as an exact percentage in the Evidence column.

Don't write down a high number just because you really believe your thought could be true. The goal is to estimate the likelihood objectively, not to rate how likely your thought feels. If you find that you're basing the probability of something happening on how anxious you feel, then your likelihood estimate is probably too high.

3. Now ask yourself, How do I know that this has happened or might happen? Under your likelihood estimate, list all the evidence for and all the evidence against your original anxious thought. Remember to look at all of the available evidence instead of focusing only on evidence that supports your conclusion. You can do this by asking, Is there any evidence to the contrary that I might have overlooked? Keep asking yourself these questions to get as accurate an estimate as possible.

To gather evidence about a future prediction, look for related facts from the past. During this exercise, Stacy realized that she was basing her prediction "I will not have my degree four years from now" on her difficulty keeping up with the reading for her history course. But when she looked back at her past class performance, she realized that she had fallen behind in her course readings before and always passed her classes.

4. Now that you've examined the likelihood and the evidence for your original anxious thought, go back over each alternative in the Alternatives column and follow the exact same procedure. Estimate the likelihood for each alternative and write this percentage down. List all the evidence for and against each alternative that you can.

During this process, you may realize that you still have overestimated the likelihood of your original specific anxious thought. If so, go back and adjust your first likelihood estimate each time you suspect that this is the case.

5. After examining all of your alternatives in this way, go back and see which ones are more likely than your original anxious thought. Rank each alternative, as well as your original anxious thought, from most to least likely.

6. Take any specific action you might have discovered during this process:

   - If your anxious thought is a prediction about a future outcome, is there anything specific you can do to make a more desirable outcome more likely? If at any point during this process you discover a solution to a concrete problem at hand, go ahead and act on it.

   - If your anxious thought reflects an interpretation of something that has already happened, is there anything you can do to verify your likelihood estimates? Sometimes you can gather evidence about a worry by simply asking the right person the right question.

7. At the end of each week, go back through your journal and see how accurate your likelihood estimates were. Track the actual outcome of your worries and see how often the outcomes you worried about happened. How often did an alternative happen instead? For those instances

when your original prediction did happen, how well did you cope with it? Gathering evidence about the outcome of your worries as events unfold can be very enlightening.

Step 4: Suppose the Worst Did Happen

What if you work your worry through these first few steps and still have that nagging feeling? You may have realized that what you're worried about is unlikely, but the fact that it still could happen or could have happened is haunting you in the back of your mind. The goal of this next step is to follow your worry all the way through and face it down directly. In this step, you'll ask yourself what would happen if your original anxious thought was true. But unlike worry, where you only ask this question rhetorically, you'll push yourself to answer the question objectively.

When we're caught up in a worry spiral, we blow the outcome way out of proportion. Over a short period of time, molehills become mountains. We trick ourselves into believing that if what we're worried about did actually happen, it would be a disaster of catastrophic proportions. We expect that we'd be unable to cope with it and can't even imagine what we might do. This keeps us from remembering all the times in the past when we handled life's problems as best we could.

We also fail to see that sometimes an outcome we wouldn't have hoped for ends up leading to something wonderful. This reminds me of a close friend from high school who was devastated when she was rejected by her top college choice. She ended up going to her second-choice school, where she met the love of her life, and has since achieved everything she hoped for in her professional work. To this day, she and her husband celebrate that college rejection! Think back over your own life and see if you have a similar story. Can you remember a time when what you were worried about did happen and it led to something completely unexpected?

PERSPECTIVE EXERCISE 4: Suppose the Worst Did Happen

1. Make a column labeled "Suppose the Worst" just to the right of your Evidence column.

2. Rewrite your original specific anxious thought from the first column in this one.

3. Place a downward-pointing arrow underneath this thought as you ask yourself, If this did happen, what would happen next? Write your answer to this question underneath the arrow, then draw another downward-pointing arrow beneath it.

4. In response to this second line, again ask yourself, If this did happen, what would happen next? Write your answer under the arrow, and question this response in the same way. Keep going until you feel you've hit your final feared outcome and you can't think of the next response.

5. Go back over each line in the worry chain you have just written. Starting at the top with your original anxious thought, ask yourself these questions for each line:

- So what if it did happen?
- What would I do if that happened?

- What would I do to handle the situation?

- How would I cope with it?

- How have I coped with similar situations in the past?

- What about that outcome would be so awful?

- What would happen next?

Write your answers to these questions below your worry chain in the Suppose the Worst column.

6. Now it's time to go back and generate alternatives for each line in your worry chain. Next to your answer in the second line of your worry chain, write down at least two other outcomes that could result if your original anxious thought actually happened. You've probably come up with one of the worst possible outcomes already, so these alternatives should include a fairly neutral outcome and a surprisingly desirable outcome.

7. Now do the same for the next line in your worry chain. Think of at least two alternative outcomes for each line and write them next to that line in your worry chain. As you do so, ask yourself these questions:

- Which of these three possibilities is most likely?

- How would I cope with each possibility?

The idea of this exercise is to see the infinite number of possibilities that could arise even if your original specific anxious thought occurred. It also gives you the opportunity to see that you have the strength to cope with the worst of these, even if all the outcomes in your worry chain were to happen.

Step 5: Explore New Perspectives

The goal of this final step is to pull together all of the careful thought and hard work you have done in the previous four steps. Now that you've really examined this worry objectively, it's time to find a new perspective that is more balanced and flexible. Your new perspective should incorporate all the shades of gray that fall between the black and white extremes. This means that you see your situation with fewer expectations and assumptions about it, rather than being convinced of your original view with complete certainty.

PERSPECTIVE EXERCISE 5: Explore New Perspectives

1. Make one last column at the far right and label it "New Perspectives."

2. Read over all of your writing from the first four steps. Ask yourself these questions:

- What have I discovered about myself and my worry that I hadn't realized before?

- What other ways of looking at my situation had the greatest impact on me?

3. Summarize this information into a sentence or two and write it in the New Perspectives column. Your summary should reflect a new perspective that is more objective and balanced than your original specific anxious thought.

After you've had some practice with all of these exercises, go back through your journal and look for themes. Try to remind yourself of your new perspectives as you catch your worry spirals during your daily monitoring.

DISCOVER THAT YOU DON'T NEED TO WORRY

Worry is a catch-22 for many women. It leaves them feeling wound up, on edge, and filled with self-doubt. But at the same time, a part of them secretly believes that they need their worry to manage their lives and ward off disaster. They feel stuck in a never-ending double bind, caught between a rock and a hard place. For this reason, many women find worry to be the lesser of two evils.

Why do women believe they need to worry? What possible advantages do they see in worry when they're constantly suffering the disadvantages? For many women, worry doesn't feel like a conscious choice that is under their control. It's as if the mind has a "mind" of its own, determined to keep worrying regardless of the cost. Here's why: the vast majority of times you worry about things, they don't end up happening. But instead of learning that you might as well not have bothered to worry in the first place, your mind makes the mistake of assuming that your worry somehow prevented something bad from happening. If you're usually worrying about something, then you seldom get to experience that nothing bad would have happened in the absence of worry. The same outcome probably would have occurred even if you never gave it a second thought. So your mind hangs onto worry as a strategy to prevent the next disaster coming down the pike.

Here's a list of common beliefs about worry from a Penn State research study:[*]

- Worry helps motivate me to get things done that I need to get done.

- Worrying is an effective way to problem solve.

- If I worry about something, when something bad does happen, I'll be better prepared for it.

- If I worry about something, I am more likely to actually figure out how to avoid or prevent something bad from happening.

- Worrying about most of the things that I worry about is a way to distract myself from even more emotional things, things that I don't want to think about.

- Although it may not actually be true, it feels like if I worry about something, the worrying makes it less likely that something bad will happen.

If any of these sound familiar or if worry feels uncontrollable for you, you can break this cycle. Examine these beliefs by treating each one as an assumption and taking it through all the steps you've learned in this chapter. Here are some considerations to keep in mind as you examine each of them:

[*]   Reprinted from *Journal of Behavior Therapy & Experimental Psychiatry*, vol. 26, Borkovec and Roemer, Perceived functions of worry among generalized anxiety disorder subjects: Distraction from more emotionally distressing topics? pp. 25–30, copyright 1995, with permission from Elsevier.

Gain a New Perspective

1. Look for evidence by comparing a time in your life when you worried a lot to a time when you hardly worried at all. Were you really better off when you worried to anticipate every little thing?

2. When a situation turned out better than expected following worry, wouldn't that same outcome have occurred even if you hadn't worried about it?

3. Isn't it possible to effectively solve problems without worrying about them first?

4. Aren't there other ways to motivate yourself without the anxiety and distress of worry, such as rewarding yourself as you accomplish certain tasks?

5. Usually it's adaptive to be aware of your *current* surroundings. See if you're missing any important information from the present moment while your thoughts are elsewhere worrying. You'll learn some strategies to help you with this in chapter 7.

As you take your worry beliefs through the five steps you've learned in this chapter, weigh the negative costs of excessive worry against the benefits you perceive. What are the disadvantages of holding onto these beliefs about needing to worry? In addition to all the distress it causes, worry keeps you from discovering that you can cope with situations and manage your life without it.

CHAPTER 5

Face Your Fears

THE PROBLEM WITH AVOIDANCE

When you worry, you're thinking a lot about the things you fear. But your mind spins around the issue without really facing your fears down. You've already started to face your fears by taking your worries through the steps in the previous chapter. You explored your thoughts by getting your worry specific, considering alternatives, examining the evidence, considering the worst-case scenario, and exploring new perspectives. Your efforts at examining your automatic thoughts and gaining a new perspective will really pay off if your behavior backs them up. In this chapter, you'll learn to confront fears directly by acting differently.

Changing your behavior is an important part of turning worry spirals around. When you give in to that urge to avoid certain things, you strengthen your hidden beliefs that those situations are threatening and that you really might not be able to handle them. In fact, the simple act of avoiding something can make it become scary. You probably could create all sorts of new fears just by purposefully avoiding things you aren't afraid of now.

Avoidance behavior gives your worry extra momentum. If you avoid certain situations because you're worried about the outcome, you never get to learn what would have happened if you had faced those situations. You deprive yourself of the chance to see how you would have coped. When you decide to avoid, you experience a temporary state of relief. But you're also left feeling powerless and deflated, as if you can't control your own behavior. Eventually you become discouraged and disheartened as a vague sense of feeling paralyzed sets in. This is how avoidance slowly eats away your self-confidence over time.

As you practice each of the exercises in this chapter, remember that the goal is not to feel comfortable. In fact, each exercise is designed to help you venture out of your comfort zone. Push yourself to feel vulnerable—this allows you to learn that you can handle whatever happens. It's important to realize that even the most difficult of emotions can't destroy you. We're all capable of feeling intense fear so that we can escape life-threatening situations. Occasionally you might feel the urge to avoid something that is truly dangerous, and in this case, your avoidance behavior protects you exactly as it should. But usually people avoid things that make them feel uncomfortable, not things that can kill them.

Finally, remember that courage is about acting in the face of fear, not living without it. As the well-known psychologist Stanley Rachman pointed out (1990), courage is taking action despite feeling afraid, not acting in the absence of fear. Be on the lookout for any self-defeating thoughts suggesting you're a coward or a weak person because you have difficulty entering situations other people don't fear. Instead, you can view yourself as courageous with each practice, no matter how it goes.

BEHAVE BRAVELY: HOW TO FACE WHAT YOU AVOID

The exercises in this chapter will help you pin down exactly what you avoid. You'll learn how to purposefully approach your feared situations one at a time, a strategy called *exposure*. You'll start with the most manageable exposure tasks then try more and more challenging ones as you gradually work your way up. Instead of being inhibited, you'll soon enjoy feelings of mastery and empowerment.

Identify Specific Situations You Avoid

Before you can face your fears, you need to figure out exactly what you might be avoiding. This can be tricky for worriers because their fears rarely center on just one or two topics. Perhaps you fear actual objects, situations, or activities that many people fear. Heights, air travel, snakes, and visiting the dentist are all common examples of phobias. Any progress you make in confronting these specific fears can boost your self-confidence and prepare you to face the situations that are closely tied to your worries.

Social situations and interactions are a good place to look for avoidance behavior. Maybe you avoid social gatherings in which you have to face a lot of people or meet new people. If you worry a lot about what other people might think, often feel afraid that someone won't like you, or spend your energy trying to please others, then you are probably avoiding certain social interactions. Obvious examples include attending parties, dating, going out to dinner with people, striking up conversations, and taking the initiative to socialize with people. But many women also avoid more subtle social interactions. Expressing your opinion, standing up for yourself, giving a friend honest feedback, and disclosing intimate or private details about yourself to a loved one are all good examples. Be on the lookout for any time you feel yourself holding back with other people.

Another good place to look for avoidance behavior is your worry itself:

- What situations do you avoid because of your worry?

- Do you avoid saying no or making requests of other people because you're worried about what they'll think?

- Do you avoid watching the news, reading the paper, or listening to the radio, afraid you'll only find more to worry about?

- Do you avoid watching certain movies because they stir up deep emotion?

- Do you avoid driving when you've just heard about a car accident?

In the previous chapter you may have discovered situations in which you could have asked someone for feedback to gather evidence about your worry. See if you can identify any instances in which approaching someone or something would have given you a clearer picture about whether or not your worry was justified. Include any situations that, had you faced them, would have given you information that may have put your worry to rest.

One final word about facing situations that you fear: If your instincts are telling you that a certain situation or person really could be physically dangerous, don't go against your common sense and good judgment. The exercises below help you face things that make you feel uncomfortable in order to overcome the fears and worries that are holding you back. This is very different from avoiding real danger for your protection. Walking alone down a dark alley in the city, confronting a family member who has hurt you physically, or approaching an ex-boyfriend who has threatened to harm you are the types of situations to avoid for your personal safety.

FACING FEARS EXERCISE 1:
Identify Specific Situations

1. Pull out a new sheet of paper and brainstorm about all the activities and situations you avoid because they make you uncomfortable. Make three columns on the page. Label the first column "Phobias," the second column "Social Situations," and the final column "Daily Activities." List each situation or activity that you avoid in the appropriate column. Be sure to write down anything that's already come to mind from your reading so far.

2. Look over this table of common situations and activities people avoid and identify which ones apply to you. Add any of these that apply to you but are not yet on your list in the appropriate column.

Phobias	Social Situations	Daily Activities
Snakes or spiders	Talking to people	Watching, reading, or listening to the news
Other animals	Meeting new people	Driving
Heights	Asserting yourself	Traveling away from home
Air travel	Parties	Leaving kids with a babysitter
Elevators	Meetings	
Dentist	Dating	
Needles	Public speaking	

3. Next, go back through your worry journal entries. Try to identify any scenarios or social exchanges you took steps to avoid or almost avoided. Really take your time with this, listing as many as you can. If you later remember things you didn't think of at first, just add them to your list. Keep adding to this list as you discover other situations you're tempted to avoid.

Create an Exposure Ladder

Now that you've found some specific situations you avoid or are sometimes tempted to avoid, it's time to rank them in order from the easiest to the most daunting. If you've discovered that you avoid a number of things here and there, you might be feeling a bit defeated, wondering how you'll ever be able to tackle them all. It *is* too overwhelming to consider confronting all the situations you avoid as one huge task. Instead, you'll start at the beginning with the most manageable situation first. Once you feel you've conquered it, you'll move on to the next one. This one-step-at-a-time approach is very important.

Often people find that once they start facing even the easiest of their avoided situations, the difficult ones start to look much more doable. That's because they build up momentum as their confidence grows. Don't get discouraged if you have a lot of situations to confront. As you embrace your new goal of facing your fears, each time you approach a new situation you'll be turning around a potential worry spiral. This new way of living will start to take hold, and your long-term goal of approaching the remaining situations will seem more and more possible.

FACING FEARS EXERCISE 2:
Create an Exposure Ladder

1. Go back over the list you created for the first exercise in this chapter and rate each item for difficulty. For each, ask yourself how anxious that activity or situation would make you feel. Use the same 0 to 100 anxiety rating scale from chapter 3 that you use for your daily monitoring.

2. Once you've rated each situation or activity on your list, rearrange them in order from the lowest anxiety rating to the highest. If you have a lot of these, you can rewrite them in rank order on another sheet of paper.

3. On a separate sheet of paper, draw a wide ladder with as many rungs as the number of situations and activities you came up with in the previous exercise. It's best to do this exercise in pencil—this will make it easy for you to go back and rearrange. If you really went all out and came up with a lot of situations and activities, go ahead and group similar types of situations together.

4. Write the situation or activity with the lowest anxiety rating on the bottom rung of your ladder, the next lowest on the second rung, and continue up the ladder in this way until you have all of your situations or groups of situations worked into the ladder. If all of your situations have high anxiety ratings, look for easier versions of them to include on the lower rungs. For example, an easier version of the high-anxiety situation of asking your boss for a raise could be asking about her weekend next Monday. Your ladder can even include situations or activities you already do but feel apprehensive about when you do them.

Confront Each Fear, One at a Time

Now you're ready to face the situations on your hierarchy, climbing up your exposure ladder one rung at a time. You'll select one situation for exposure practice and plan ahead exactly when and how you will confront it. When it's time to enter the situation or do the activity you have planned, remember to allow all the feelings that come with trying something new and scary. Don't try to fight them off with a hidden goal of feeling comfortable. On the other hand, approaching your exposure practice as if you're holding on for dear life only strengthens your original anxious beliefs. That's why "white-knuckling it" will only undermine your efforts. You may have already discovered this if you've confronted some of these situations in the past only to feel worse about them afterward. Instead, you can embrace the discomfort and excitement of trying something new with a sense of pride and courage.

During the exposure practice itself, be aware of what you're saying to yourself about it. Is your mind working to convince you that you can't handle the situation or the feelings of fear and other difficult emotions? It's important to watch your thoughts, all the while reminding yourself that they are only thoughts. This will help you experience the situation in a new way instead of just rehearsing all the threatening interpretations that come to mind automatically.

FACING FEARS EXERCISE 3:
Confront Each Fear, One at a Time

1. Pick a situation or activity from the bottom rung of your exposure ladder.

2. Figure out exactly where, when, and how you will attempt to confront it. This will vary a bit depending on the situation. For example, one woman might decide to start with a social situation such as striking up a conversation with a particular person at work. In another case, a woman afraid of driving might decide to drive an extra block out of her way instead of taking her usual route home from the grocery store.

3. When the time comes, follow through with your plan by approaching the situation or activity directly. Immediately beforehand, rate your anxiety using the 0 to 100 anxiety rating scale.

4. As you experience the exposure, stay focused on all that is actually happening around you and within you as best you can. Stay in the situation as long as you can—until you have completed what you set out to accomplish or until the situation comes to its natural conclusion. Immediately afterward, rate your anxiety level again.

5. Repeat this entire exposure practice again at a later time. Keep repeating it until that activity creates only minimal anxiety for you, with a rating of 10 or less on the anxiety rating scale.

6. If your anxiety doesn't start to go down after several attempts, carefully examine how you might be unintentionally rehearsing your anxious beliefs. What are you telling yourself about your practice or your ability to do this that's left you feeling worse? Following through with your practice and getting anxious is *not* failing. Remember the goal is to feel uncomfortable, not comfortable. The only way to fail at this exercise is to not do it in the first place—if this happens, all you need to do is try again. Perhaps you're trying to do too much too soon.

Pick an easier variation of the activity to make it more manageable. For instance, let's say you planned to strike up a conversation with your boss at work but didn't follow through when the time came because you felt too overwhelmed. Before trying to approach this particular situation again, you might try to strike up a conversation with a coworker instead. Remember that success with these practices comes when you muster up the strength to actually do them; how other people react is neither here nor there.

7. Once you have mastered the bottom rung of your exposure ladder, move up to the next rung. Follow these exact same steps:

- Plan out exactly where, when, and how you will confront it.

- Follow through with your exposure practice as planned, rating your anxiety beforehand and afterward.

- Repeat your exposure practice until the situation no longer makes you very anxious (about 10 on the anxiety rating scale).

- Keep moving up your exposure ladder in this way one rung at a time.

GO BEYOND YOUR COMFORT ZONE

Confronting the specific situations you fear and avoid is certainly important. But you can take the spirit of your exposure exercises a step further by approaching new and unfamiliar situations as you come upon them. You'll enjoy an extra confidence boost and prevent future avoidance behavior if you stay on the lookout for new things to try from time to time.

Can you think of something new and different you've always wanted to do, but for one reason or another you just didn't bother? Sometimes the simplest changes in routine can make a difference if they nudge you out of your comfort zone. Enrolling in that class you've always wanted to take, ordering something new at your favorite restaurant, trying out a new leisure activity or hobby—these are the kinds of things that add some variety to life and keep us on our toes. Whenever you find yourself playing it safe by sticking to what's familiar, push yourself to do something different. As you encounter new experiences or opportunities and feel apprehensive, ask yourself if there's any real harm in trying them. If not, go ahead and give them a try. The less you cling to rigid routines and habits, the more flexible you become. Plus, you'll prove to yourself that life can be filled with choices and options rather than ruled by doubts and fears.

GIVE UP WORRY SPIRAL BEHAVIOR

In addition to avoiding certain situations and activities, many worriers do certain things to feel safe. Although you feel better in the short term, you also strengthen underlying beliefs that you need to worry. This can sabotage your efforts at turning your worry spirals around. Common examples include checking things, arriving very early for appointments, calling loved ones to make sure they're okay, or asking other people for reassurance repeatedly.

Regina: Superstitious and Frazzled

Take the example of Regina, a twenty-five-year-old new mother from Kansas. Regina's husband was required to travel almost every month, about a week at a time, for his sales job in electronics. Regina always dreaded the day he left on a trip. Each time, she found herself home alone with their new baby girl, filled with worry. As soon as he left it would begin: *What if he misses his plane? What if the hotel lost his reservation? What if he forgets his briefcase at the hotel and finds himself at his sales meeting unprepared?* Regina learned to cope with her worry by calling her husband each time she figured she could reach him. She called him on his cell phone to make sure he was on the plane, again at the hotel's check-in time to make sure he got a room, then several times the next morning to remind him to take his briefcase. She became more and more eager to get him on the phone, holding out for that precious feeling of relief that came from knowing everything was okay.

On one trip, Regina's husband forgot to recharge his cell phone battery before he left, and his phone fell dead before he even got to the airport. When Regina discovered she couldn't reach him, her worry spiraled to new heights. She spent the entire day miserable and frazzled, struggling just to take care of her daughter. Eventually her husband called from the hotel, only to be chewed out for being so careless. Regina hung up the phone in tears, wishing she knew how to turn things around.

With the help of a therapist, Regina learned to take steps to let go of this particular worry behavior. She began with planned exposure practices in which she could only call her husband twice per day. She called at times that were sched-uled in advance rather than calling when she felt an impulse to be comforted. Instead of working herself up into a worry spiral, she practiced examining her thoughts and began trusting that her husband would cope with whatever problem came up as best he could. Regina tracked what happened when she called her husband and compared this to the times when she didn't call him. She discovered a strong belief that somehow her calls protected her husband from disaster—even though she never considered herself a superstitious person. Eventually, Regina was able to call her husband only once a night when he traveled. Instead of worrying about him, she enjoyed the time alone with her daughter and looked forward to her husband's return.

Maybe this story sounds familiar, or maybe it's reminded you of your own worry spiral behavior. Push yourself to go without this safety behavior for a certain period of time and see what happens. What do you think would happen if you don't triple-check something or get reassurance from your friends about your worry? This is a prediction to examine using the strategies you learned in chapter 4. Conduct experiments in which you compare times you did the worry behavior to times you didn't. Of course you'll feel uncomfortable at first, but what actually happened? And what price are you paying to feel that short-term relief? Regina discovered that her worry behavior was not only contributing to her worry spiral, it was also keeping her from having a meaningful conversation with her husband when they did talk.

As you give up your own worry spiral behaviors, you'll free yourself from worry spirals and keep them from fully developing. Plus, you'll have more energy to spend doing what you really value in your life.

CHAPTER 6

Relax Your Body and Mind

THE BENEFITS OF RELAXATION

By now you've had some practice tracking the thoughts, feelings, sensations, and behavior that make up your own unique worry spirals. Each time you catch a spiral early, you're able to nip it in the bud and turn the process around. In chapter 4, you learned to overcome the anxious thoughts that pop up when you worry, and chapter 5 taught you how to tackle worry spiral behaviors and triumph over urges to avoid certain situations. Now you'll learn relaxation strategies for the physical sensations and subjective feelings of chronic tension that worriers often experience.

Worry and muscle tension go hand in hand. Have you ever noticed a sore back or a headache at the end of a stressful day because you were clenching certain muscles without even realizing it? Muscle tension creates a number of physical effects, such as feeling like your stomach is tied up in knots, heavy breathing or sighing, and gastrointestinal symptoms, including diarrhea, nausea, and constipation. There are psychological side effects too. Tension fuels worry spirals, making it easier for your mind to get swept up in your anxious thoughts. It's much easier to take life as it comes when you're living in a general state of relaxation. Think back to a period of time when you felt particularly relaxed. Wasn't it harder for worry spirals to take hold?

The purpose of this chapter is to teach you specific relaxation skills that will help you go through life more relaxed. The goal of regular relaxation practice is to lower your overall baseline level of tension. Another important goal is to develop these skills so you can apply them quickly, as soon as you catch yourself in a worry spiral. You'll learn to relax your muscles directly, to create relaxing mental images, and to breathe in a way that relaxes both the body and the mind. It's best to try all of these, practicing each one faithfully for a while before you decide which ones work best for you. Don't be surprised if one relaxation technique takes longer to get the hang of than the others.

WHEN NOT TO USE RELAXATION

Most anxiety experts agree that relaxation should not be used to dampen the feelings and sensations of fear during exposure exercises. In fact, many think you need to experience the full fear response and let it run its natural course in order to learn that the situation you're facing is not actually threatening. This goes for all the exercises in chapter 5. Attempts to relax out of desperation will probably just backfire anyway. Relaxation doesn't work as a magic cure to save you from your emotions. In fact, relaxation is a paradox: the harder you try to relax, the less likely you are to succeed at it. Think of times when you felt like you absolutely had to relax. How well did your efforts really work?

However, it can be quite helpful to apply relaxation techniques to cope with stresses and strains throughout your day. Whenever you're having difficulty deciding whether to use your relaxation skills, honestly answer the following questions:

- Do I want to relax to feel calmer and more centered so that I can deal with the situation in front of me and experience it more fully and openly?

- Or am I only trying to save myself from uncomfortable feelings of fear?

If you answer yes to the first question, go ahead and give relaxation a try. But if you answer yes to the second question, allow yourself to feel your fear rather than trying to relax it away.

Practice your relaxation skills regularly on a day-to-day basis. Soon you'll be able to use them to calm yourself throughout your day, especially when you catch a worry spiral developing.

BREATHE SLOWLY AND DEEPLY

Breathing is a little peculiar: We absolutely have to do it to stay alive. Therefore, we can breathe automatically without any awareness at all, such as when we're asleep. Then again, we have a lot of voluntary control over how we breathe when we're awake. Because breathing is so basic and automatic, most people develop habits of breathing a certain way at a particular baseline rate without ever noticing it. Physical activity as well as stressful events certainly can change these breathing patterns for a short time. But some people chronically breathe just a little bit faster than their bodies need. They also tend to take shallow breaths mostly from their chest. This is especially true for people prone to anxiety and worry. The subtle effects of this slight overbreathing build up over time. Hyperventilation eventually results, dramatically affecting both the body and the mind.

Usually people are breathing from some combination of their chest and their stomach. Breathing from the chest affects the body one way, while breathing from the stomach has an entirely different impact. That's why slow and deep stomach breathing is such a simple yet powerful relaxation technique. When you breathe mostly from your chest, the part of your nervous system that increases your arousal and heart rate gets stimulated. Plus, you use mostly your chest muscles to do the work. Your chest muscles are not really designed for breathing the way that certain abdominal muscles are. In instances of extreme chest breathing, people will even feel sensations of tightness or pain in the chest as these muscles get tired.

On the other hand, taking deep breaths from your belly stimulates the branch of your nervous system linked to slowing the body down, resting, and relaxing. Your heart rate slows down, and food absorption becomes easier for your digestive system. This kind of breathing uses an abdominal muscle called the *diaphragm*, a large curved muscle located near the bottom of your rib cage. Some people call this breathing relaxation technique *diaphragmatic breathing* because the diaphragm is the muscle best equipped for breathing. Have you ever seen a baby or a young child breathe while sleeping on his or her back? The breath starts way down in the belly, which fully expands, resulting in a slow, flowing, continuous motion.

The goal of this relaxation technique is to get your body back to breathing this way. Don't be surprised if this takes some effort and patience. You may have some very strong chest-breathing habits to break. With enough practice, you can develop a new habit of slow and deep stomach breathing. You can also create the habit of checking in with your breathing frequently, then immediately shifting to diaphragmatic breathing if your breaths are fast, shallow, or erratic. And finally, this is a great way to turn around a worry spiral when you pick up on it during your regular monitoring.

RELAXATION EXERCISE 1:
Breathe Slowly and Deeply

1. Put one of your hands on your chest and the other hand on your stomach. Continue breathing naturally. Which of your hands is moving? Are they both moving to some degree? This is a quick and easy way to see how much you normally breathe from your chest versus your stomach.

2. Next, try to shift your breathing so that only the hand on your stomach moves. Keep the hand on your chest as still as possible. Imagine taking each breath all the way down to the bottom of your stomach. With each inhalation, your belly should expand. If this isn't working, purposefully push your stomach out a bit just before you inhale. This will create a space for the air coming in. Keep your belly as relaxed as you can. Feel free to take your hands off your chest and abdomen as you get the hang of breathing this way.

3. Keep your breathing smooth and fluid. Let the air come in gradually and evenly throughout each inhalation. Don't take a full breath all at once at the very beginning of the inhalation. Likewise, allow the air to escape gradually and evenly as you exhale. It might help to breathe only through your nose, imagining the air slowly leaking out your nose as you exhale. You can also try pausing for a brief moment between each inhalation and exhalation.

4. At least once a day, practice this breathing technique for about ten minutes. Twice a day is best. Each practice session should take place where you can sit or lie down comfortably without anyone or anything to disturb you. For most people, it helps to close their eyes to minimize outside distractions.

5. Begin each practice session by breathing normally. Tune into the sensations and experience of breathing this way, noticing how much of your breath is coming from your chest versus your stomach. Then shift your breathing to your stomach as much as you can. Focus your attention on keeping each breath smooth and fluid.

6. As you continue this diaphragmatic breathing, keep your breaths slow and regular. For most people, a slow breathing rate falls somewhere between eight and ten breaths per minute. Experiment with your breathing rate a bit to see what's best for you. To do this, count to four silently to yourself with each inhalation then count to four again with each exhalation. If this is too long, try counting to three instead.

Continue counting and breathing in this way for the full ten minutes of practice.

7. If your mind wanders off during this practice, just gently bring it back to your breathing and counting. Pay attention to the sensations that come from breathing in this way.

RELAX YOUR MUSCLES

Muscle relaxation techniques have been around for a very long time. Back in the 1930s, physiologist and physician Edmund Jacobson discovered that his patients didn't startle very much when their skeletal muscles were relaxed. The opposite seemed to happen too. Have you ever noticed that you're particularly jumpy when your muscles are tense? Jacobson believed that chronic muscle tension was the source of many medical complaints among his patients. So he developed an elaborate procedure to teach his patients how to relax individual muscles one at a time in a deliberate and systematic way. This *progressive relaxation* technique was first published about seventy years ago (Jacobson 1938). A few decades later, psychologists Douglas Bernstein and Thomas Borkovec (1973) streamlined the original Jacobson procedure, making it much simpler and easier for people to use. Just like the original procedure, people learned to purposefully tense then release certain muscles to relax them systematically. This abbreviated method was recently expanded and updated (Bernstein, Borkovec, and Hazlett-Stevens 2000). In this next exercise, you'll learn an even simpler brief muscle relaxation procedure to practice.

Why does it help to tense your muscles before relaxing them? It's important that you become aware of muscle tension sensations so you can learn how to reduce tension by letting go of it. We all carry around a certain amount of muscle tension every day. If certain muscles weren't tense enough, we wouldn't even be able to stand up or hold our heads upright. But many people have developed the unconscious habit of tensing certain muscles although they don't need to do so for physical posture or movement. Or maybe they carry around much more muscle tension than they need over the course of the day.

As you practice, you'll tense each muscle group first to gain some momentum. This will help you release the built-up tension completely. Plus, your mind will learn to tell the difference between the two sensations. With practice, you'll become better and better able to distinguish between the slightest bit of tension and complete relaxation. You'll eventually practice scanning your body for extra tension and letting it go right then in that moment without going through the tension and release cycles.

Getting Started

The exercise in this section will teach you how to tense and release different muscle groups during your practice sessions. Here are some guidelines to follow during each muscle relaxation practice session:

Get comfortable. Find a comfortable place in your home, such as a bed, couch, or reclining chair, where you can practice for about fifteen to twenty minutes free from distractions. Wear loose and comfortable clothes. Remove your watch, shoes, eyeglasses, and any jewelry that puts pressure on your body, such as a tight necklace or ring. Dim the lights in the room a little.

Avoid disruptions. Plan ahead so you aren't interrupted by the phone or the doorbell. Ask the people you live with not to disturb you. Make a trip to the bathroom. It's also a good idea to schedule your practice sessions for a time when you have nothing else to do immediately afterward. This will allow you to focus your full attention on your relaxation practice without concern for when you finish.

Don't overdo it. Each time you purposefully tense a muscle group, you should be able to notice a clear difference between this muscle tension and relaxation. But this doesn't mean to tense your muscles as much as you possibly can. Certain muscles, especially in the calves and the feet, can cramp easily. Produce just enough tension to feel the contrast between muscle tension and relaxation without going overboard. Of course, if you have a medical condition involving your muscles, you may not be able to tense and relax certain muscle groups. If you have any concern about such physical limitations, be sure to check with your doctor before trying the muscle relaxation exercises.

Keep still. Try not to move your muscles, especially after you've relaxed them. It's okay if you need to shift your body weight or scratch an itch to get comfortable. Otherwise, try to avoid any fidgeting or unnecessary movement.

RELAXATION EXERCISE 2: Muscle Relaxation

Practice at least once daily for fifteen to twenty minutes. Twice a day is better and will help you build your skills over a shorter period of time. During your practice, work your way through each group of muscles, one at a time and in the following order. Here's how to tense each group of muscles:

Face: Furrow your brow to create tension in your forehead as you squint your eyes and wrinkle your nose. Clench your jaw.

Arms, neck, and shoulders: Hold both arms out in front of you with your elbows bent. Clench both fists as you push down with your elbows. You should feel tension through your hands, wrists, lower arms, and biceps. Tighten up your neck and throat as you shrug your shoulders.

Chest and stomach: Tighten your chest muscles as you hold your breath and suck in your stomach.

Thighs: Raise both of your legs slightly while also trying to push them down with the muscles on top. You should feel tension throughout the upper part of your legs.

Lower legs and feet: To create tension in your calves and feet, flex your feet and pull your toes back as you curl or crunch your toes. Don't tense these muscles for longer than five seconds at a time and be careful not to cramp.

Now you're ready to begin. You might want to close your eyes. Follow these steps for each muscle group:

1. Create tension in only that muscle group and hold it for seven seconds.

2. As soon as your seven seconds is up, immediately release all muscle tension.

3. Study the difference in sensations now that these muscles are relaxed.

4. Enjoy these sensations for the next thirty to forty seconds before moving on to the next set of muscles.

5. Repeat the sequence of muscle groups in this way two to three times during each practice session.

Carefully focus your full attention on the physical sensations of tension and relaxation throughout your practice session. Really study them and notice the contrast between the two. If you catch your mind wandering off, just bring it back to your practice session and the physical sensations in the muscle group you're working on.

Don't be alarmed if the relaxation sensations feel a bit new and unusual—if you're often tense, it might take some practice just to get used to feeling relaxed. And don't get discouraged if this relaxation technique takes a lot of practice at first.

As you begin to practice, it might be difficult to remember which muscle groups to tense and how to tense them. If you're having difficulty with this, you might want to slowly read the exercise instructions into a tape recorder first. Start by reading the instructions for how to tense the muscle group, wait seven seconds, then instruct yourself to relax these muscles for thirty to forty seconds before moving on to the next muscle group. Then you can listen to your tape to guide you through your practice sessions. Just be sure that you don't become dependent on your tape to relax. As soon as you learn the routine, stop using the tape. This will ensure that you develop relaxation skills without needing to rely on an audiotape.

RELAX YOURSELF THROUGH IMAGERY

Creating mental imagery is a powerful ability we all possess. We can create our own unique virtual reality without any special equipment at all! Why is visualization or imagery so potent? Unlike thinking in words, this type of mental activity is closely tied to our emotions. Have you ever noticed that picturing something happening in your mind stirs up deeper feelings than just thinking about it verbally does? This is why people feel such intense fear when they imagine something catastrophic happening. It's almost as if the situation were actually happening or at least becoming more likely to happen than it was before. Here's the good news: You can use this same ability to visualize pleasant scenarios that relax you deeply. Try the exercise below to put yourself into a relaxing scene as fully as you can. With practice, you'll take less and less time to become absorbed in your imagery and achieve a state of deep relaxation.

RELAXATION EXERCISE 3:
Visualize a Relaxing Scene

1. Come up with a specific scene linked to feelings of peace, calm, pleasure, and relaxation. This could be an actual place you've visited, a far-away place you've seen on television, or somewhere that exists only in your imagination. For most people, this involves a place of natural beauty in the outdoors. Settings such as the beach, a green meadow, a field filled with a favorite type of flower, a forest, or the open desert are some examples.

2. Find a place where you can sit or lie down comfortably without being disturbed for the next five minutes or so.

3. Close your eyes and turn on the image you've chosen. Visualize your scene vividly, with as

much detail as you can. What colors and sights do you see?

4. Include your other senses in your imagery as much as you can:

   - What fragrances do you smell in the air at your scene? If you're imagining yourself on a beach, try to smell the salt of the ocean. If you're in a forest or up in the mountains, try to smell the scent of pine. If you're in a meadow or a field, smell the fragrance of flowers or grass.

   - What sensations can you feel on your skin? The warmth of the sun? A gentle breeze?

   - What sounds do you hear in your scene? The movement of the ocean waves? The chirping of birds? The rustling of the wind?

5. As you stay in your scene, experience it as vividly and fully as you can. Notice how your body feels as you sink into a deeper and deeper state of relaxation. After your five minutes are up, give yourself a moment to enjoy how you feel before getting up and going about your day. Try this exercise once a day for at least a week, as well as anytime you have a spare moment to relax.

APPLY YOUR RELAXATION SKILLS

You've now learned three separate relaxation skills to help you reduce your overall levels of tension. Once you've had enough formal practice sessions to get the hang of them, you can relax yourself whenever you pick up on a worry spiral during your regular monitoring. You can also develop habits of relaxing throughout the day. One way to do this is to schedule mini breaks throughout your day. During these short breaks, retreat to a quiet place to practice any of these three relaxation skills for just a few minutes.

You can also relax your muscles and shift to deep breathing right in the moment whenever you want. Try the following exercises to remind you to relax and keep you relaxed throughout your day.

RELAXATION EXERCISE 4:
Develop Relaxation Response Habits

1. Think of your two or three most common anxiety habits:

    - Do you frequently bite your nails?

    - Do you sigh heavily under stress?

    - Do you fidget in a certain way, such as twirling your hair, tapping your fingers, cracking your knuckles, or picking at your skin?

2. Be on the lookout for these as you monitor your anxiety and worry throughout the day as you learned in chapter 3. Whenever you catch yourself doing these, shift to a relaxation response.

    Check your breathing: Are you breathing quickly or mostly from your chest? If so, shift to slow and deep stomach breathing. Continue your diaphragmatic breathing as long as you can.

Scan your body for extra muscle tension: Be on the lookout for unnecessary muscle tension, especially those muscle groups most likely to be too tense. Let go of this tension as best you can, relaxing all extra muscle tension away.

RELAXATION EXERCISE 5:
Find Relaxation Reminder Cues

1. Every day contains dozens of hidden moments to relax. The trick is to plan ahead so you can identify these situations as reminders to relax. Here are some examples:

- Waiting in line at a store or bank
- Sitting in your car at a red light
- Watching a commercial on television
- Waiting for your computer to boot up
- Waiting for a pot of water to boil
- Walking to or from your parked car
- Waiting for your kids while picking them up at school

2. Pick two or three of these that work best for you. Each time you find yourself in these situations, let them remind you to relax. Follow the same steps as in the previous exercise: Check your breathing and shift to slow and deep stomach breathing. Then scan your body for any extra muscle tension and relax the extra muscle tension away.

CHAPTER 7

Focus on the Present Moment

WHY FOCUS ON THE PRESENT?

There are many benefits to paying attention to what's going on inside of you and around you in the moment. The present is all that truly exists at any point in time—the future hasn't happened yet and the past is over. The present moment is your window into what's really happening right here and right now. Noticing how you really feel about something can guide you to do what's right for you. Taking in all that's occurring around you allows you to respond to what's actually happening in front of you as events unfold. This is quite different from reflexively reacting to a situation based on assumptions and automatic habits from the past.

So what does paying attention to the present moment have to do with worry? The two are incompatible. Worry usually involves thinking about things that could happen in the future or have happened in the past. This necessarily keeps you from fully experiencing the present moment. You can't be completely focused on the present when you're thinking about the future or the past. When you worry, at least some of your attention is spent interpreting past events or creating an illusion about the future. You might miss important information coming from your surroundings that actually exist right in front of you in that very moment. Not only might you miss the potential joy and excitement that moment might bring, but you may also be missing important information from inside yourself or from the immediate environment to guide your behavior. Can you think of any times that you missed something useful in the present moment because your mind was distracted by worry?

WHAT IS MINDFULNESS?

Every person's mind tends to wander off to the past or the future, regardless of how much they usually worry. This is just a natural human tendency, probably because of the usefulness of being able to evaluate the past and anticipate the future. But making a special effort to experience the present moment and become aware of your wandering mind can interrupt worry spiral habits dramatically. When you're purposefully paying attention to your present-moment experience, you also become aware of your automatic reactions. This intentional and careful way of experiencing the present moment is often called *mindfulness*.

The goal of mindfulness practice is to bring your attention back to the present moment whenever you notice your mind wandering off. You've already started developing this skill with your relaxation practice in the previous chapter. But mindfulness is more than simply focusing your attention on the present moment. It also means being patient with yourself during the process and allowing yourself to experience the present moment as fully as you can. As you become more and more aware of your thoughts, feelings, and bodily sensations, also practice *not* reacting to them. The tendency is to instantly judge an experience as good or bad and to push away bad experiences and hold onto good ones. The two main goals of mindfulness practice are first, to become fully aware of the present moment, and second, to welcome and allow all experiences to come and go naturally instead of judging them or trying either to hold onto them or push them away. You can also practice bringing your mind back to the present moment whenever you catch a worry spiral developing. This can help break your automatic worry spiral habits.

Practice mindfulness on your own using the exercises described in this chapter. If you'd like to read more about it and learn additional ways to practice, see the Resources section. You might even decide to take a yoga or meditation class.

MAKE MINDLESS TASKS MINDFUL

One way to practice mindfulness is to pay full attention during the most mundane and simple activities you do every day. This is a good place to start because these activities have already become highly automatic. When was the last time you fully experienced brushing your teeth, taking a shower, or washing the dishes? Probably back when you were a child first learning how to do these things. Each of these activities creates a wide variety of physical sensations and sequences of movement we rarely notice anymore.

Sometimes it's efficient to do simple routine things automatically to free our minds up for complex problem solving and creative thinking. But constant multitasking comes at a price. When you do most things automatically, you set the stage for unwanted habits, such as worry spirals, to become automatic too. It becomes more and more difficult to slow down and tune into the present moment.

PRESENT MOMENT EXERCISE 1: Everyday Tasks

1. Find a routine activity that you do every day without thinking, such as brushing your teeth, taking a shower, washing the dishes, or washing your face.

2. Over this next week, each time you do this activity take special care to perform it mindfully. Make a conscious and deliberate effort to bring moment-to-moment awareness to even the smallest step of the activity. Pay attention to all of the physical sensations of touch, smell, sound, sight, and taste throughout the activity. The goal of this exercise is to focus in on exactly what you're doing as you are actually doing it.

3. Really experience every nuance of this activity. If you selected brushing your teeth, experience how the toothbrush bristles feel against different parts of your mouth and gums, the taste of the toothpaste, and how the water splashes against the roof of your mouth. For washing dishes, notice the temperature and feel of the water against your hands, the smell of the soap, and the texture of the bubbles. As you can already see, mindfulness is nothing fancy or mysterious. It's simply a different way of being that you can practice at any time just by choosing to pay attention to the present moment, no matter what you happen to be doing at the time.

4. As with all mindfulness practice, bring yourself back into the present moment as fully as you can whenever you notice your mind wandering off. Becoming aware that your mind has wandered off and bringing it back to the present is just as valuable as staying focused on the activity.

EAT MINDFULLY

Eating is another everyday activity most people do automatically without paying attention. When was the last time you slowed down enough to really taste your food? Of course we have to eat regularly to stay alive. This makes it easy for us to develop automatic habits around eating too. In the next exercise, you'll practice eating in a slow and deliberate way, noticing even the slightest facet of how the food looks, smells, and tastes. Because people rarely eat mindfully, this mindful eating exercise might feel strange. If mindless eating is an issue for you or if you find this exercise particularly helpful, you might want to read *Eating Mindfully* by Susan Albers (see Resources).

PRESENT MOMENT EXERCISE 2: Mindful Eating

1. Select a certain meal or a specific time that you eat a snack each day.

2. Sit down and eat your food where you can focus all your attention on the experience of

eating without being distracted. Make sure your television or stereo is turned off.

3. Before putting the food in your mouth, take the time to look at it carefully as an observer, almost as if you were seeing this food for the first time. While noticing its colors, shading, surfaces, and texture, also notice its smell. Become aware of any thoughts and feelings about food that might come up. Pay attention to any physical sensations of feeling hungry or feeling full.

4. Allow yourself the time you need to eat very slowly, observing the appearance and aroma of each bite before you carefully and intentionally bring the food up to your mouth. Really notice the taste and sensation of having each bite in your mouth, swallowing only when you consciously decide you're ready. How does the texture of this food feel on your tongue? What sensations do you notice while swallowing?

5. As you notice any thoughts, feelings, and sensations during your mindful eating, also notice your mind's tendency to judge your experience. Whenever you notice your mind wandering, simply take note of your thoughts, trying not to judge them one way or another, and bring your mind back to the present moment experience of eating.

6. How does this way of eating compare to how you usually eat? Challenge yourself to eat at least once a day in this fashion. Don't get discouraged if this feels a bit unusual—it might

take several days or even a few weeks before this way of eating starts to feel natural.

BREATHE MINDFULLY

Breathing is one of the most fundamental things we do. Luckily, our bodies are programmed to breathe automatically to keep us alive. But this also means we're rarely aware of our breathing in a mindful way. In chapter 6, you tuned into your breathing patterns as you learned to breathe in a relaxing way. In this next exercise, the goal is not to change your breathing so much as to fully experience the act of breathing itself. The movement and sensations of breathing can become a powerful focal point for your mind as you practice mindful awareness.

PRESENT MOMENT EXERCISE 3: Mindful Breathing

1. Find a place where you can sit upright or lie on your back comfortably. Free yourself from distractions, such as the telephone, the television, and other people.

2. As you close your eyes, focus all your attention on your breathing. Feel the air enter your body as you breathe in and follow it as it moves down into your stomach. Feel the sensation of your stomach expanding and then falling as you begin to exhale.

3. As you stay in the moment of each breath, focusing all your attention on the full length of

each inhalation and exhalation, your mind will undoubtedly start to wander. When you notice this, just gently bring your awareness back to your breath.

4. When people first begin this practice, they often become concerned about whether they're doing it "right." Surely there must be something more to this than just sitting and watching your breaths! This exercise is very simple yet difficult at the same time. We're so accustomed to "doing" something each moment of our lives that taking time out to just sit can feel downright peculiar. But the simple act of making time each day to be with your breathing without an agenda can be quite powerful.

5. Practice mindful breathing in this way for at least ten minutes a day for a full week and see what happens. With practice, you'll be able to check in with your breathing at any time throughout your day to anchor yourself.

MAKE LEISURE ACTIVITIES MINDFUL

When you're busy with a hectic life and feeling stretched too thin, leisure time feels like a luxury. But taking just a little time out once in a while to do something you really enjoy is important for your body, mind, and spirit. What do you most enjoy? Creating or viewing art? Listening to a certain type of music? Gardening, golfing, baking, or playing the piano? Give yourself the gift of leisure even if you don't have much time to spare. During this activity, practice mindfulness by experiencing each moment as fully as you can, tuning into all of the sensations and movements involved.

PRESENT MOMENT EXERCISE 4: Leisure Activity

1. Pick something you love to do that would be possible over the next week. If you can't come up with anything, pick a favorite piece of music. Listen to this music as your leisure activity until you get the chance to try other things.

2. Each time you do this activity, experience each moment as it unfolds, just as you have practiced in the previous present moment exercises. Immerse yourself in it as much as you can. Make each movement conscious and deliberate. Take in all the sights, smells, sounds, and sensations as you experience them.

3. Each time you notice that your mind has wandered off, gently bring yourself back to the present.

PART III

OVERCOMING
SPECIFIC WORRIES

CHAPTER 8

Worry About Relationships

RELATIONSHIP WORRIES

Relationships and social interactions are what people worry about most, regardless of whether they struggle with chronic worry (Roemer, Molina, and Borkovec 1997). This probably isn't surprising to you. After all, we human beings are social animals. We live in a very interpersonal world where other people's anger or negative judgments about us can carry real consequences. Plus, none of us can ever completely read another person's mind and know what they're thinking or feeling. This leaves each interpersonal exchange at least a little hazy.

Relationship worries often surround a fear of others' disapproval or rejection. Themes of wanting to please others or care for others can also lie at the heart of these worries. Sometimes relationship worries lead to avoidance of certain social situations, especially those where you expect other people might judge or evaluate you in some way. More subtle avoidance includes giving in to demanding requests, not asserting yourself, and not letting other people know what you really want or feel. Relationship worries and social avoidance behavior can crop up in relationships with a variety of people, ranging from your coworkers and your boss to your partner or spouse, family, and close friends.

Understanding your worry can be very tricky in the context of relationships. That's because some worry spiral behaviors actually jeopardize the quality of the relationship itself. These worries are very difficult to let go because they contain a grain of truth. For some people, expressing their worry becomes their main way of letting others know they care. Over time, they gradually lose touch with other ways of showing and expressing their love. Anne's story is a good example.

Anne: Unwittingly Pushing Others Away

Anne, a forty-five-year-old married mother of two teenage boys, worked part-time as a legal assistant in a small law firm. She was very active in the school's parent-teacher association and volunteered weekly at the community women's resource center. Anne enjoyed being involved in her community and raising her sons, but her worry about others was always on her mind. When talking with her husband, sons, or friends, much of Anne's energy was spent scanning them for cues to gauge how they were really feeling. Out of concern for their welfare, she would repeatedly question them to make sure they were really okay. Anne would openly express how worried she was about them, often second-guessing whether they'd be able to handle life's disappointments.

Anne began to notice that her husband and close friends were pulling away. She discovered that a group of her friends got together without her. Her husband was initiating sex less and less often, and he no longer came home from work excited to tell her about his day. Her sons were getting more and more annoyed with her—it seemed as though she couldn't say a word without them rolling their eyes. Anne quickly became consumed with worry about her relationships: *Why don't my sons appreciate all that I do for them? How could my friends exclude me like that? Does my husband even love me anymore? What if he's having an affair? What if he asks me for a divorce?*

As Anne's relationship worries began to spiral, she sought reassurance from others. She asked her husband ten times in one night if he really loved her. She called each of her friends twice a day to make sure she would be included the next time they met for coffee. Anne also felt increasingly frustrated with her sons. It seemed as though they didn't appreciate or respect her at all anymore. One evening she yelled at the boys like she never had before when they came home late from their friend's house.

When she felt like she'd had enough, Anne decided to turn things around. She learned to examine her relationship worries in an objective and systematic way. She discovered that she was underestimating herself as well as others. This had eaten away at her self-confidence and pushed her loved ones away. Anne realized that she was interpreting every little nuance and facial expression from others as a sign that something might be wrong. This kept her from really hearing what the other person was trying to say. Plus, it led her to assume that others were disappointed and disapproving of her. This left Anne feeling resentful, lonely, and hurt, as if no one really understood her.

Anne mustered up the courage to get a dialogue going with her husband. One night when she felt that familiar urge to ask him if he really loved her, she opened up instead and talked about her fears. She asked him how he really felt about their marriage and how her worry was affecting him.

Although Anne's husband first responded with his usual reassurance, he soon disclosed that he missed the way things used to be between them. Anne actively listened as her husband described the impact her worry behavior was having on him. A part of her was surprised to hear that he was feeling just as lonely and isolated as she was.

Anne's new approach spread to her other relationships. Anne made an effort to stay focused in the present moment when talking to her friends or her sons. She cut back on seeking reassurance and checking to make sure others were alright. She created an exposure ladder and began to confront other interpersonal situations one step at a time. As she examined her relationship worries, she discovered which beliefs about relationships were useful to her and which ones weren't. Instead of waiting for a gesture of appreciation from her sons, she took steps to care for and reward herself.

If you worry about relationships or social situations, Anne's story might sound somewhat familiar. But maybe not—relationship worries and the behavior that results can differ dramatically from person to person. Anne was outwardly very social and expressive about her worries. Perhaps you're much more shy and afraid of meeting new people in the first place. Many chronic worriers also fear and avoid a wide range of social situations. They're regularly concerned about what others will think of them and worry about saying or doing something embarrassing. This particular type of anxiety and worry is called *social anxiety* or *social phobia*. If you suspect that extreme shyness or social anxiety might play a role in your relationship worries, use this chapter to apply the strategies you learned in part 2. If you'd like more help with this particular problem, try some of the additional resources listed in the back of this book.

Regardless of the nature of your relationship worry, this chapter will help you examine your worries carefully to gain a new perspective, provide some specific ways to face your fears, and help you apply your relaxation and mindfulness skills in this area of your life. You can even photocopy the table at the end of this chapter to carry with you—it will prompt you through each of these strategies as you catch yourself worrying about relationships.

GAIN A NEW PERSPECTIVE

In chapter 4, you learned five specific steps to examine your worries carefully and put them into a new perspective. You started with a vague worry and narrowed it down to a concrete and specific prediction or interpretation (get specific). Next, you brainstormed about other possibilities (generate alternatives) and examined the likelihood of your anxious thought as well as your alternatives (look at the evidence). You then learned to take an honest look at what would happen if your anxious thought occurred and how you would cope (suppose the worst did happen). Finally, you found a new perspective that was more balanced and flexible yet less anxiety provoking than your original anxious thought (explore new perspectives). Here are some suggestions that might be particularly helpful as you practice putting your relationship worries into perspective.

Step 1: Get Specific

As you challenge yourself to get as specific as you can, transform your vague relationship worry into a very concrete interpretation or prediction. This might involve a specific interpretation of what another person is thinking or a prediction about how they will respond in a particular situation or circumstance. Be on the lookout for labels and stereotyped terms. For instance, if you're predicting that someone will "act like a jerk" or "be mean" to you, exactly what are you predicting will happen? How will that person behave such that an outside observer could say whether or not your prediction came true?

Step 2: Generate Alternatives

As you consider alternative interpretations or outcomes, push yourself to come up with different ways in which *you* might respond to the situation. Worries about relationships and other people often involve a focus on what the other person might think, feel, or do. This can lead to feelings of powerlessness, as if the other person has complete control over the interaction and maybe even the whole relationship. This makes it very difficult to see your own contribution to the social exchange and discover how you might be able to turn things around.

Step 3: Look at the Evidence

Take a careful look at how you arrived at your conclusion about this interpersonal situation:

- Are you assuming your interpretation or prediction must be true because it feels true?

- Are you making snap judgments about what someone else must be thinking or feeling?

- Are you convinced that your take on things is the only possibility?

- What evidence from your past experiences goes against your conclusions?

Sometimes people make the mistake of expecting that everyone else will think, feel, and react to a situation in the same way that they would. But this type of expectation is rarely based on concrete evidence. Stick to the facts and what has or hasn't actually happened. If you discover that you don't really have much evidence either way, that's important to keep in mind too. Instead of replaying your anxious thought over and over in your head, wait and see how things actually turn out.

But what if you carefully look at the evidence and come to realize that what you're afraid of is quite likely? What if your prediction is actually very realistic? When looking at the evidence, it's also important to examine your own contribution to the social interaction at hand. You might be carrying around certain expectations of others that actually make your feared outcome likely. Relationship worries aren't always based on a hasty jump to conclusions. They also can reflect hidden expectations about how other people should behave that are just plain impractical. Many people have firm beliefs about how relationships should work. Sometimes these beliefs are helpful, sometimes not. For example, it's very sensible to expect loved ones to treat you with a certain level of respect. But it might be worth taking a second look at other personal beliefs or relationship rules that might set you up for disappointment, such as trying to change other people, not asking for what you want, taking care of others but not yourself, asking who's to blame, and wanting to be right every time.

Stop Trying to Change Other People

Some people secretly believe they have the ability to change someone else. They hope beyond hope that if they just push hard enough and keep at it, the other person will someday see the light and be transformed. On the one hand, it's quite reasonable to expect that you can influence other people. If you let them in on what you want or need, they're often willing to oblige. But the chances that your friends, spouse, romantic partner, or parents will change lifelong habits because of you are probably fairly slim. They might give in for a short time if you pressure them enough. But resentments soon set in on both sides, only increasing the gap between you. That's why expecting other people to change will often set you up for disappointment. Ultimately, every adult is responsible for his or her own self.

Luckily, you don't have to let your own happiness and well-being become dependent on someone else's choices. You can make your own decisions about what you want to do instead of concentrating on what you want someone else to do. Rather than focus on how you'd like other people in your life to be different, take charge over your own behavior. Make whatever changes in your own life you find meaningful.

Ask for What You Want

It's tempting to see personal relationships as if they were legal contracts. But each person has a one-sided view of how the other person should keep up their end of the bargain. So both people wind up with different assumptions about how things should go and a different definition of fairness. As soon as one person acts out of step with the other's expectations, their behavior is seen as not being fair: *If my husband really cared about me, he'd offer to do the laundry on Saturdays. If Amy was a real friend, she'd ask me out to lunch more often. If my parents valued me, they would call me instead of waiting for me to call them.*

If you're feeling treated unfairly, take a careful look at what you're expecting from the other person. Focus on what you want instead of whether the other person is being fair. This will prompt you to express your personal preferences and desires in a clear and direct way. You'll also keep resentments and bad feelings from building up. Of course the other person might choose not to grant your request. But then it's up to you to decide how you want to handle things from there.

Take Care of Yourself, Not Just Others

Do you often feel unappreciated for the sacrifices you make? For many women, taking care of other people is a big part of their daily life. Even if you don't have children, you may work in a profession that revolves around caring for others. Taking care of loved ones and helping others comes quite naturally to many people. After all, it makes us feel human, as if we're part of something greater than ourselves. But altruism can turn sour if you neglect yourself in the process. As people become aware of their personal sacrifices, they start to expect recognition, rewards, and appreciation from the world around them. Often they aren't even aware of this expectation. They only notice themselves becoming more and more bitter and resentful, waiting for something that never seems to come.

Instead of suffering for the sake of others, create your own rewards. Stop taking on responsibilities that only leave you feeling resentful in the end. Take steps to nurture yourself as well as you nurture everybody else. You've already started by reading this book! If you find yourself becoming bitter, remember that you are your only caregiver. Nobody is more responsible for your health and well-being than you are. In the end, it's a win-win situation: the more you take care of yourself, the better you're able to care for others.

Don't Bother Asking Who's to Blame

When people feel disappointed or hurt in a relationship, it's tempting to figure out who's at fault. They get caught up with blame, deciding who's responsible for their situation or their feelings. Blaming someone else keeps you from seeing your own role in the exchange. Blaming yourself leads to self-defeating thoughts and keeps you from holding the other person accountable for their own choices and behavior.

The way around this blaming trap is to take responsibility for asserting your own needs and making your own choices. Taking responsibility is quite different from simply turning the blame on yourself. You can accept the consequences of your actions without attacking yourself in the process.

You Don't Have to Be Right Every Time

Do you sometimes find yourself on the defensive? In some interpersonal situations, people feel as though they have to prove themselves to others. The desire to have the correct answer and show why your view of the world is best can become almost intoxicating. But this gets in the way of looking beyond your own opinion and taking in new information from others. It also builds a wall between you and the other person.

If you find yourself in this position, remind yourself to take a step back and listen. Don't just hear the other person's words in order to prepare a brilliant comeback. Really listen in an active way with the goal of understanding the other person as best you can. There's no loss if you consider the other person's viewpoint valid or even change your mind. Having the guts to admit when you're wrong can really pay off in your relationships.

Step 4: Suppose the Worst Did Happen

Now that you've taken a careful look at the evidence and examined your own relationship expectations, ask yourself what would it matter if your anxious thought did happen: What if the other person doesn't like you and has a negative opinion of you? What if your friend, partner, or parent is angry or upset with you? What if last night's date isn't interested in a second date?

- What exactly would happen next?

- What concrete steps would you take to cope with your situation?

- What does this mean about you as a person?

If you're expecting to get through life pleasing everybody or never feeling embarrassed, you're in for a rough ride. Take an honest look at the weight you give other people's approval of you. Of course it's useful to impress other people. An ability to get along with others will serve you in countless personal and professional relationships. But you won't pull it off 100 percent of the time. That's why it's useful to ask yourself how you would cope. Remember that all emotions—even feelings of hurt or embarrassment—are temporary and will pass. If you do embarrass yourself in front of others, how long will the embarrassment last? How will you feel about it the next day, the next week, or next year? Will it really be such a big deal then?

Maybe some of your worries are about your close intimate relationships. When faced with the possibility of relationship conflict, it's easy to take things personally. But people who love each other also get angry with each other and work to resolve their conflicts.

Step 5: Explore New Perspectives

As you create a more balanced view of relationships, adjust any expectations of yourself and of others that might not be working very well. Don't create a new perspective that leaves you hoping other people will react to you in a certain way. Instead, incorporate any helpful realizations that came up during this process. This might include reminders that you can't please everyone all of the time, that feelings of embarrassment will pass, or that you can cope with others' criticism and disapproval.

FACE YOUR FEARS

In chapter 5, you learned how to create an exposure ladder and confront the situations you avoid in a step-by-step way. If you worry about relationships, you might be avoiding certain social situations or interpersonal exchanges. Do you worry about what other people think of you? If so, try to approach social situations that make you feel uncomfortable. You might start with something simple, such as striking up a conversation. You could then move up to inviting a friend to lunch. More difficult situations to try next might include asserting your opinion or making a request of another person. As you take on more and more challenging social situations, you might eventually work your way up to asking your boss for feedback on a work project or giving a presentation to a group. If everyday social situations tend to make you very uncomfortable, you might want some extra help confronting them. See the social anxiety resources at the back of this book for more guidance.

Create Intimate Moments

Many worriers avoid intimacy in their close personal relationships. Even if socializing with other people isn't a problem, you still might avoid talking about certain topics with a loved one. Be on the lookout for moments when you hold back sharing what you really want, think, or feel. Here are a couple of specific exposure practices you might want to try:

1. Approach your partner, spouse, or a close friend for a heart-to-heart talk. Ask openly and directly what impact he or she thinks your worry behavior has had on your relationship. If your loved one tries to reassure you, let him or her know that you would really appreciate honest feedback. Probe for ways in which you might be pushing the other person away or coming off as distracted, overbearing, or nagging. As emotional and difficult as this may be, actively listen to how the other person feels. Allow yourself to feel vulnerable as you discuss your struggle with worry and anxiety and disclose your deepest fears about the relationship. The goal of this exercise is not necessarily to solve any problem. Instead, just practice truly being yourself with your loved one in as genuine and authentic a way as you can.

2. Are you currently married or in a close romantic relationship? If so, start a dialogue about what each of you enjoys most in the bedroom. Discover ways of communicating your own preferences to your partner. Summon up the courage to initiate sex or to try something new. If this seems a bit daunting, check out the books *Sex Talk*, by Aline

Zoldbrod and Lauren Dockett, and *Sex Matters for Women*, by Sallie Foley, Sally Kope, and Dennis Sugrue (see the Resources section for more information on these books). Both are chock full of practical suggestions and exercises to help you explore and enhance your sex life.

What if your relationships don't really allow for open and honest communication? What if you try these things but your partner or friends aren't willing to support you? It might be time to work on building your social support network. Surround yourself with people who are safe to talk to and willing to listen. Meet new people by getting involved in something you care about in your community. You might even want to attend local support group meetings.

Give Up Relationship Worry Spiral Behavior

Which worry spiral behaviors are you most prone to do when you worry about relationships? Do you ask someone for reassurance over and over again? Do you double-check to make sure the other person is not mad at you or still loves you? Look for anything that might be creating distance in your relationships. Anne, for instance, discovered a number of worry spiral behaviors, including checking with others to make sure they were okay, asking her husband if he loved her, and calling her friends repeatedly to ask when they were meeting for coffee.

Consider sharing your efforts with significant others. Let them know what changes you're trying to make in your life and how you're learning to turn your worry spirals around. See if you can come up with helpful ways the other person could respond when you express a certain worry or start a worry spiral behavior. The other person might have developed habits of responding to you that give you short-term relief but keep the worry process going. Each time you ask the other person for reassurance, he or she could fight the urge to reassure you and instead support you in working through the perspective exercises in chapter 4. Each time you feel an urge to do a worry spiral behavior, you don't have to give in. Instead, let the urges serve as cues to remind you to relax and bring your mind back to the present moment.

RELAX YOUR BODY AND MIND

In chapter 6, you learned some specific relaxation skills to apply throughout your day as you catch your worry spirals developing. Regular practice of these skills might also pay off in your relationships. It's much easier to take a step back and listen to what another person is saying when you're calm. Just think of times in the past when you got in an argument with a loved one. Were you already wound up and stressed out before the conversation even began? How might you have responded differently if you approached the situation feeling centered and relaxed?

FOCUS ON THE PRESENT MOMENT

You learned how to practice mindfulness during everyday activities such as eating and breathing in chapter 7. See if you can practice being fully present as you interact with other people. Each time you notice your mind wandering during a conversation, bring it back to what's going on in front of you at that moment. What is the other person really saying? How do you feel in each moment as you talk to that person? As you create intimate moments with your loved ones, experience the feelings of intimacy and vulnerability as fully as you can.

Gain a New Perspective

Get Specific

- Avoid labeling the other person.
- Predict specifically how he or she will behave.

Generate Alternatives

- List different ways both of you might respond.

Look at the Evidence

- What are you assuming about the other person?
- Check for any impractical expectations:
  - Stop trying to change others.
  - Ask for what you want.
  - Take care of yourself.
  - Don't bother asking who's to blame.
  - Remember you don't have to be right.

Suppose the Worst Did Happen

- How would you cope with conflict or others' disapproval?

Explore New Perspectives

- Adjust expectations of yourself and others.

Face Your Fears

- Confront social situations and assert yourself.
- Create intimate moments with significant others.
- Stop worry spiral behaviors, especially seeking reassurance.
- Teach loved ones how to support you.

Relax Your Body and Mind

- Practice regularly to reap the relationship benefits.

Focus on the Present Moment

- When your mind wanders, bring your attention back to the conversation.
- Experience the other person in that moment as fully as you can.

CHAPTER 9

Worry About Work and Achievement

WORK WORRIES

Achievement can become a double-edged sword. As children we learn early on that if we work hard and stay determined, we can achieve wonderful rewards down the road. As parents we strive to instill a work ethic in our children, wanting them to learn the value of setting and achieving goals so they become productive members of society. But what happens when we take these values so far that success at work, work productivity, and the achievement of tangible rewards starts to define our worth as human beings? This is a common trap for people who often worry about work, school, and achievement.

In the first half of the 1900s, women typically worked in their homes. As women became liberated to pursue their own intellectual and occupational interests outside the home, they discovered many of the same pitfalls men were dealing with in the professional world. Of course, women also experience their own unique set of challenges in the workplace.

Women today face tough decisions about balancing their work with their family responsibilities, although more and more men are struggling with these issues as well. We've come a long way as a society, but unfortunately not all work environments encourage fair and respectful treatment of their female employees. These problems can add an extra layer of complication for working women. But this doesn't mean that women are less capable of overcoming obstacles at work or less able to create fulfilling careers for themselves.

Joan Borysenko (1996) describes an important transition in women's lives when they reevaluate their life's work and their earlier life decisions. Some women might find their career is not working out as planned once they've achieved their initial career goals. Others might realize that their choice to work full-time caring for their family at home is not measuring up to their ideals. As you examine your work worries, see if they reveal any useful information about your own life decisions and values.

Work worries involve fears of failing at work, not getting work done, your work not being good enough, not working hard enough, or, alternatively, suffering the consequences of working too hard. If work, school, or achievement is a common worry topic for you, use this chapter as a guide to apply the strategies you learned in part 2. You can even photocopy the table at the end of this chapter to carry with you—it can prompt you through each of these strategies as you catch yourself worrying about work.

GAIN A NEW PERSPECTIVE

In chapter 4, you learned five specific steps to examine your worry in a new way and gain a new perspective. First, you learned to take a vague worry and narrow it down to a concrete and specific prediction or interpretation (get specific). You then brainstormed about other possibilities (generate alternatives) and examined the likelihood of your anxious thought as well as your alternatives (look at the evidence). Next, you learned to take an honest look at what would happen if your anxious thought occurred and how you would cope (suppose the worst did happen). Finally, you found a new perspective that was more balanced and flexible yet less anxiety provoking than your original anxious thought (explore new perspectives). Here are some tips that might be especially helpful as you put your work worries into perspective.

Step 1: Get Specific

As you work to get your achievement-related worry as concrete as possible, watch out for general and vague terms like "failure," "success," or "good enough." How could an outside observer tell if you "failed" or if your work wasn't "good enough?" Exactly what are you predicting will happen?

Step 2: Generate Alternatives

As you brainstorm about the full spectrum of possible alternative outcomes, see if you are getting stuck on any certain aspect of your work situation. For example, are you assuming that you'll have your current job throughout your career? If so, make a point of generating alternative scenarios that involve a job change. Push yourself to come up with alternatives that aren't based on the assumption that every part of your current situation will remain fixed forever. Remember that the goal of this step is to free up your thinking and challenge yourself to think outside the box.

Step 3: Look at the Evidence

As you examine the likelihood of your original anxious thought and each alternative, remember to look for evidence against your anxious thought instead of focusing only on the evidence that supports it. Look back at your record of past performance to test your conclusions about failing to achieve something. If you're worried about failing a test in college, how many tests have you taken and how many of these resulted in an F? If you're worried about the results of a performance evaluation coming up at work, what's the nature of the feedback you usually receive in your work evaluations? Be careful not to interpret the anxiety you feel about your feared outcome as evidence that it's likely to happen.

But what if your work worries center around themes of not getting your work done on time? What if you're realistically predicting that you won't finish everything on your plate in time to meet deadlines? This was a big problem for Ellen, a woman who often found herself stuck when she got to this step.

Ellen: Overcommitted and Overwhelmed

Ellen was a single, thirty-two-year-old sociology professor at an Ivy League university. Her tenure review was only two years away. At that time, she would be evaluated by her fellow professors and either lose her job or receive a lifelong offer to stay. Ellen knew the competition was tough. She would have to produce a large number of scholarly publications and work very hard to have a fighting chance. This pressure started to weigh on her day and night. Plagued with worry about getting things done and not being productive enough, she woke up exhausted every morning. Sometimes the worry itself woke her up, leaving her haunted by a constant flow of anxious thoughts: *Oh no, it's already the 25th and this month is almost over . . . that book chapter I agreed to write is due next week . . . how am I going to get that done when I still need to get those article revisions to my editor by the first of the month?*

Ellen decided that her plan to get to the gym three times a week was impossible. She also declined an invitation to a friend's dinner party she was really looking forward to. Although she felt a bit of immediate relief, she also felt trapped by her work and wondered if she would ever feel that she could afford time for a life.

Eventually Ellen felt as though she was reaching her breaking point. As she began to track her worry spirals, she discovered that she was coping with her worries of not being productive enough by taking on *more* work projects. Instead of prioritizing her tasks at work and making deliberate choices about how to spend her precious work time, she wasted energy working haphazardly while worrying about all the other projects she wasn't working on at the moment. Her worry spiral behavior of committing to new projects she didn't have time for was actually increasing her chances of missing deadlines and feeling overwhelmed.

Ellen examined her worry by breaking it down to one specific instance at a time and generating alternative outcomes. But she often got stuck when looking at the evidence. This step always seemed to reveal that her specific anxious thoughts were actually very likely. Finishing everything she had planned within a certain amount of time was quite unrealistic, if not impossible. Ellen had created a trap for herself in which her own tendency to overcommit ensured that she would never keep up with her work. Her unreasonable expectations about how quickly she should be able to work created a self-fulfilling prophecy. Ironically, the intense anxiety and worry that resulted only weighed her down and kept her from working to the best of her ability.

As Ellen began to realize the self-defeating nature of her approach, she began to put careful thought into which work projects were best for her career goals and which ones weren't. Each day, she began her work with one specific task planned at a time. Although she felt uncomfortable turning down certain requests and negotiating deadlines with her colleagues, the payoff for both her work productivity and her quality of life was huge. Ellen came to realize that caring for her health and well-being actually allowed her to work more effectively and efficiently, not less.

If Ellen's story sounds at all familiar to you, there might be some specific behavior changes you can make to address your work worries. You'll read more about these in the Face Your Fears section of this chapter.

Step 4: Suppose the Worst Did Happen

Regardless of how realistic or unrealistic your anxious thought may be, it's always a good idea to ask yourself what would it matter if it did happen: What if you do lose your job, fail that class, miss that deadline, or get that unsatisfactory work evaluation?

- What exactly would happen next?

- What concrete steps would you take to cope with your situation?

- What have other people done when they were faced with a similar situation?

- What would it mean to you if this happened?

This last question is especially important to ask if your work worries involve themes of failure.

Fears of Failure

Failure is one of the most common endpoints to chronic worriers' worry chains, even when they start out worrying about something other than work (Hazlett-Stevens and Craske 2003). Why is the prospect of failure so scary? After all, failures are guaranteed to happen unless you refuse to take any risks. And if you aren't willing to take risks, you'll never have opportunities for success. Yet it can feel so personal to lose a job, to receive a college rejection letter, or to watch someone outperform you at work.

The difficulty seems to come when we make the mistake of equating our own personal worth with what we can achieve. It's very tempting to do this when we receive awards, accolades, or other tokens of our success. Everyone wants to feel important and good at what they do. But sometimes we get into the habit of comparing ourselves to others. When we succeed more than the next person, we feel superior. But this also means that if we hadn't, we'd be inferior. This way of thinking raises the stakes, leaving us pressured to achieve even greater success the next time. If success at work makes us more valid, lovable, and worthy human beings, then failing means we're less so. This quickly leads us down a dangerous road, paralyzed by a fear of failure.

But here's the good news: You can liberate yourself from this catch-22. You can choose not to measure your fundamental worth by what you achieve at work. You can stop comparing yourself to other people. Although it's humbling, putting your achievements and failures into perspective frees you up to take whatever risks seem worth taking. This allows you to take pride in your work and enjoy your successes for what they are.

What can you do if failure is a common theme in your work worries? You can compare the importance of your work to the importance of other things in your life. Ask yourself questions like these:

- How important is this work worry compared to my health, my family, and other important people in my life?

- If things don't work out as I want, can I still have a rich and fulfilling life?

- If I don't perform well, will the people I love most love me any less?

- If I fail, can't I still take pride in the courage it took to have tried in the first place?

- What do I value most about a person? Is it really stuff like how smart they are or how successful at work they are?

Step 5: Explore New Perspectives

As you consider perspectives that take your new insights into account, don't simply hope for things to happen that are beyond your control. Instead, focus on what you can do, how you would cope, and what your feared outcome would actually mean if it did happen. Do you suspect that you worry about work as a distraction from more difficult life issues, such as a lonely marriage or a painful experience? If so, deal with these problems directly. For example, you can work on your relationship by expressing yourself openly to your partner or looking into couples counseling. You can recover from a painful life experience by working through unresolved emotions with a good therapist.

FACE YOUR FEARS

Many different worry spiral behaviors go hand in hand with work worries. In Ellen's case, she discovered a behavior pattern of overcommitting, often taking on more work than she had time for as she worried about not being productive enough. If you suspect that you overcommit, try some of the behavior changes described in the next section.

Other common work-related worry spiral behaviors include perfectionistic checking and time-urgency behaviors. *Time-urgency behaviors* are anything you do when you're in a hurry, like repeatedly checking your watch, fidgeting, tapping your feet or your fingers while waiting in line, sighing heavily, or driving aggressively or speeding in traffic. As you catch yourself overchecking your work or doing any time-urgency behaviors, challenge yourself to go without these for the rest of the day and see what happens. You can even conduct a personal experiment and track how efficiently you work without them. In addition, the urge to do these can serve as a cue to remind you to relax and bring your mind back to the present moment.

Avoidance of certain activities and situations is another big part of work-related worry spirals. Procrastination is a classic example, in which people put off working on something out of fear for how it will turn out or how long it will take to complete. If you procrastinate, try some of the strategies described below, in the Pitfalls of Procrastination section. Also look for other ways you might be holding back, such as putting off looking for a better job, not asking for a promotion, not applying to your top college choice, or turning down work opportunities you consider worthwhile.

Finally, look for avoidance of leisure activities and of anything else you do to take care of yourself. Ellen, for instance, not only engaged in the worry spiral behavior of overcommitting; she also put off working out and socializing with her friends. What pleasant activities and ways of caring for yourself do you avoid when you're worried about work? Make an effort to schedule these into your day or your week, just as you schedule appointments and activities at work.

In chapter 5, you learned how to identify specific avoidance behaviors and gradually confront the situations you fear with an exposure ladder. You also learned how to give up worry spiral behaviors, such as repeated checking. Here are some specific behavior changes to try if you worry about work, school, and achievement.

Stop Overcommitting

So what can you do if you tend to overcommit at work? You can begin by forcing yourself to stop and think before taking on any more responsibilities. This will give you the chance to decide whether you truly have the time and whether taking on this project is in your best interest. At some point, this will probably involve saying no. For some women, overcommitment results from their fear of asserting themselves and declining others' unreasonable requests. This really can be difficult if the person making the request is your boss or someone in a position of power over you. But you can practice effective ways of telling your boss that you have more work demands than you can meet. This might include asking what responsibilities should take priority or offering to problem solve with him or her about how to best spend your work time. You can then follow through by creating a clear work plan and sticking to it by working on tasks one at a time in order of priority.

If you avoid situations such as saying no or approaching your boss for help, come up with a list of specific behaviors along these lines that you can do. Place these on your exposure ladder, with the least daunting one at the bottom and the most difficult one at the top. As you learned in chapter 5, decide exactly how and when you will try the activity on the bottom rung, follow through with your exposure practice as planned, and work your way up the ladder. You might even want to practice by role-playing with a friend first and getting some feedback.

Another helpful behavior change for people who tend to overcommit is to delegate work tasks to others. This might be difficult if you have perfectionistic tendencies. You might be afraid that other people won't do things a certain way or think they can't be trusted to do the job well enough. But you can confront these fears by deliberately delegating certain tasks or parts of tasks. If you have coworkers who share your workload or people who work for you, push yourself to ask them for help or to find tasks to delegate to them. Challenge your assumptions that you have to do everything yourself or that even the most mundane work tasks must be done to perfection.

The Pitfalls of Procrastination

Almost everyone procrastinates from time to time. Why is it so tempting to put work off? Worries about whether the finished product will be good enough can be a part of it. But procrastination also reflects our basic human nature. The most fundamental part of our brain is designed to seek pleasure and avoid what's unpleasant, and work isn't always fun. In spite of this, we often push ourselves to work even if we don't feel like it, knowing that it'll be worth it later.

But sometimes people give in to the temptation to procrastinate. Like any other avoidance behavior, the mere act of putting work off can make it seem increasingly scary and set the stage for any self-defeating thoughts to run amok: *Will I really be able to do this? What if it doesn't turn out well? What if it's just not good enough?* Your self-confidence begins to erode. Plus, the more time passes as you procrastinate, the less time you leave yourself to actually do the work. You soon become painfully aware of this, so you begin promising yourself you'll start tomorrow. Although this brings some short-term relief, you also feel powerless, as if you can't even control your own behavior. Any doubts you had at the beginning have now grown to gigantic proportions. And what once seemed like a reasonable and manageable task now appears to be the size of Mount Everest!

So how can you turn this vicious cycle around? Start by breaking the whole task down into small concrete steps. Runners don't prepare for their first marathon simply by running twenty-six miles at once. Instead, they begin with a series of much shorter runs and build up their endurance according to a carefully planned training schedule. Rather than focusing on the entire marathon distance, they approach each day by running the distance planned for that day.

What is the easiest part of your work task that you can start *today?* Create an exposure ladder with the specific actions needed to get you started working, just as you learned in chapter 5. Begin with the easiest and least daunting part of the task. Your exposure ladder should represent a concrete schedule and agenda, detailing exactly when you'll work and what you'll do during that time. Let's say you're a college student putting off your term paper. You might start by going to the library for two hours and searching the card catalogue and article databases for research material.

Follow through by committing to work on your project a certain amount of time each day. Things often take longer than we think they will, so don't be thrown if you stick to your plan but aren't progressing through the task as quickly as you had hoped. This is why it's better to set goals according to how much time you'll spend working instead of how much you'll accomplish during that time. The trick to overcoming procrastination is to honor your promise to yourself by sticking to your plan each and every day. If something comes up that gets in the way, be flexible enough to readjust your schedule and not get discouraged. Examine any anxious thoughts you notice in the process using the strategies from chapter 4.

RELAX YOUR BODY AND MIND

If you worry a lot about your work, chances are you often feel tense while in your work environment. In chapter 6, you started developing relaxation skills such as slow and deep breathing, muscle relaxation, and pleasant imagery. You also learned how to apply these skills throughout your day as you monitor and catch your worry spirals.

Take Mini Breaks

How can you incorporate relaxation practice into a typical workday? Of course, the more diligently you stick to formal home practice of exercises from chapter 6, the better these skills will kick in when you apply them in the moment at work. The trick to applying relaxation skills at work is to schedule small breaks throughout your day. Figure out exactly when you can take just five minutes at a time several times a day to unwind. Can you step away from your desk for a few minutes each hour on the hour? Or maybe you could step out into the courtyard a couple of times before lunch and a couple times in the afternoon between work tasks or meetings.

Devote these mini breaks to checking your breathing and scanning your body for any unnecessary muscle tension. Shift your shallow chest breathing to slow and fluid breaths that start way down in your abdomen, just as you learned in chapter 6. Physically let go of any muscle tension you pick up on as best you can. If it helps, you can start by purposefully tensing up that specific muscle group to create momentum right before letting go of the tension. If you have a private place to go, such as your own office or a bathroom stall, close your eyes and try one or two minutes of pleasant mental imagery. Retreat to your own peaceful sanctuary created by your mind, just as you practiced at home in chapter 6.

Use Common Events as Relaxation Reminders

In addition to quick relaxation practices during your mini breaks, be on the lookout for any mundane occurrences as you work that can remind you to relax. Whenever those reminders occur, take just a second to relax right there in that moment—to take a deep breath and relax your body. With practice you can learn to do this in a matter of seconds. For example, whenever your phone rings you could let it ring an extra time and use that moment to relax your shoulders and breathe deeply. Other instances might include each time you're walking to the restroom, dialing the fax machine, or taking a drink of water or sip of coffee.

FOCUS ON THE PRESENT MOMENT

As you develop these new relaxation habits throughout your workday, also practice bringing your mind back to the present. In chapter 7, you learned how to practice mindfulness during everyday activities such as eating and breathing. You can incorporate mindfulness skills into your workday too. As you monitor your anxiety and worry, notice when your mind is off in the future worried about your work or back in the past worrying about something that's already happened. Each time you catch your mind wandering, refocus your attention on the task at hand.

Often when we worry about work, we get caught up with the outcome of our efforts rather than the process of working itself. As you bring your mind back to the present moment, really experience what you are doing as you work. Enjoy the intellectual stimulation you get from tackling a challenging task. Allow yourself to get absorbed in the creative process. Why did you choose this line of work in the first place? For the feelings of warmth that come from helping or teaching others? For the sense of inspiration you feel when testing your own limits or learning something new? Bring yourself back to what you most enjoy about your work. Rediscover the intrinsic rewards of your work rather than worrying about whether extrinsic rewards will result in the future.

WORK AND ACHIEVEMENT

Gain a New Perspective

Get Specific

- Define general terms, such as "failure," "success," and "good enough."

Generate Alternatives

- Don't assume all aspects of your work situation will stay fixed forever.

Look at the Evidence

- Objectively examine your past performance record.

Suppose the Worst Did Happen

- Don't equate your worth with what you can achieve.

Explore New Perspectives

- Focus on what you can do and how you would cope.

Face Your Fears

- Give up perfectionistic checking and time-urgency behaviors.
- Stop overcommitting.
- Get back to leisure and self-care activities.
- Overcome procrastination by starting small and starting *today*.

Relax Your Body and Mind

- Take mini breaks throughout your day to apply relaxation skills.
- Find common events to remind you to relax at that moment.

Focus on the Present Moment

- When your mind wanders, refocus your attention on your work.
- Enjoy the process instead of thinking about the outcome.

CHAPTER 10

Worry About Physical Harm and Safety

SAFETY WORRIES

We human beings are in an awkward position. On the one hand, we have the capacity to think ahead and plan for the future. But this also gives us a unique awareness of our mortality and the possibility of losing the people we love most. We can imagine beautiful fantasies as well as horrible tragedies, knowing in the back of our minds that even the unthinkable can happen. The only certainty in life is that it will someday come to an end—for us and for each person we love. This realization leaves us feeling mortal, vulnerable, and small, wishing that we could somehow forestall the inevitable.

For some people, worry becomes an attempt to make the future more certain. If only they could foresee and prevent each of life's tragedies, then maybe they would make it through life without emotional pain, grief, or loss. Of course we always have some degree of control. Each one of us plays a very active role in our future, whether we see it or not. But at the same time, we must learn to accept the limits of our control over the world around us. Repeated attempts to predict the unpredictable and control the uncontrollable drain our energy, cause unnecessary anxiety, and keep us from experiencing the very life we hold so dear!

Safety worries typically involve predicting some sort of physical harm or injury happening to you or to your kids, family, or loved ones. Because of their tragic nature, these worries can cause powerful emotions of fear and sadness soon after the worry begins. It's also common to experience catastrophic images, in which a vivid and terrifying picture of the event pops into your mind. These images make the event seem much more real and likely, leaving you convinced it could soon happen no matter what the statistics may say. This was a common experience for Jenna, a thirty-four-year-old mother plagued by worries about her five-year-old son getting hurt.

Jenna: Imagining Disaster

In most ways, Jenna seemed like an average stay-at-home mom. She loved her son, Michael, dearly but also caught herself longing for simpler times. She looked back at her college days, marveling at how fearless and carefree she used to be. When she was eighteen, she moved across the country to attend school in New York City. Although she took a self-defense class and developed basic safety habits, such as not walking down dark streets alone, Jenna never really feared for her safety. In fact, she rarely worried about anything.

This all seemed to change the moment Michael was born. Even though Jenna lived in a safe neighborhood in suburban Connecticut, she saw potential dangers for Michael everywhere she looked. Like most new mothers, she was careful to childproof her home and check consumer safety ratings before purchasing certain products. But none of this diminished her nagging concern that an unexpected tragedy still could strike.

Now that Michael was five and playing outside regularly, Jenna's safety worries escalated to new heights. Each time she watched him play in the park with his friends, she was bombarded with vivid and graphic images of all the horrible things that could go wrong. One day she imagined Michael falling off the monkey bars and cracking his head open. Another day she envisioned Michael being hit by a car, left lying in the street bleeding. These images intruded into her consciousness and haunted her throughout the rest of the day. Jenna coped with her worry by restricting Michael's activities and hovering over him while he played. Although other mothers kidded her about being overprotective, she couldn't let go of her belief that she must anticipate every possible disaster.

If Jenna's story sounds familiar or you have similar safety worries, you might find this chapter helpful. But for some women, worry about issues of physical harm and safety reflect a currently dangerous living situation. If you're in a physically abusive relationship or are living with domestic violence, this type of situation requires you to take action to keep safe. On the other hand, women who worry about safety in the absence of immediate danger can learn to apply the coping strategies from part 2. You can even photocopy the table at the end of this chapter to carry with you—it can prompt you through each of these strategies if you find yourself troubled by worry with themes of physical harm coming to you or to someone you love.

GAIN A NEW PERSPECTIVE

In chapter 4, you learned five specific steps to examine your worry in a new way and gain a new perspective. First, you learned to take a vague worry and narrow it down to a concrete and specific prediction or interpretation (get specific). You then brainstormed about other possibilities (generate alternatives) and examined the likelihood of your anxious thought as well as your alternatives (look at the evidence). Next, you learned to take an honest look at what would happen if your anxious thought occurred and how you would cope (suppose the worst did happen). Finally, you found a new perspective that was more balanced and flexible yet less anxiety provoking than your original anxious thought (explore new perspectives). Here are some suggestions that might be especially helpful as you take your safety worries through the steps in chapter 4.

Step 1: Get Specific

Begin by identifying exactly what you predict will happen. If you discover that you can take specific action to prevent harm, go ahead and do it. For example, if you're worried about your toddler getting into poison, you can childproof your home and post the poison control number on the refrigerator. However, if you've already taken all reasonable precautions, then your worry might not be serving you.

Step 2: Generate Alternatives

As you generate alternatives, consider less dramatic, more mundane occurrences that don't lead to intense feelings. What else could happen in that situation that does not involve harm or tragedy? For example, Jenna discovered a few alternatives that were less extreme than Michael falling off the monkey bars and severely injuring his head. She came to realize that he might fall but only skin his knee; he might fall and sustain an injury that would heal, such as a broken arm; or he might play on the monkey bars without falling at all.

Step 3: Look at the Evidence

As you examine the evidence, you might find that you're overestimating how likely a particular event actually is. Maybe you think it's very likely to occur because of how scary and awful the event would be if it happened. But it's no more likely to happen just because you're thinking about it. Along the same lines, tragic events that you see on the news are no more likely to happen to you simply because you just heard about them happening to someone else. In fact, events make the news *because* they're so out of the ordinary. If you relied solely on the news to track events of the world, you'd wind up with a very selective and skewed picture. If common events were reported in the news, we'd constantly be bombarded with reports such as "Julie Smith drove home safely from work today" or "Flight 901 has just landed on time at the local airport."

Check to see if your reasoning is influenced by strong emotion. When safety worries trigger powerful images, these mental pictures make the event feel much more real than it seemed before. Visual imagery elicits deep emotion more easily than thinking in words does. Be careful not to confuse your imagery and the emotion it stirs up with evidence that tragedy is likely to happen.

Step 4: Suppose the Worst Did Happen

But what if you look at all the evidence, realize the chances are quite slim that what you fear will actually happen, but still can't seem to let go of your worry? What if the specific outcome you predict is so tragic that even a 0.001 percent chance is enough to upset you? This is why it's important to keep going and suppose the worst did happen. How would you cope with your tragic situation if it did in fact occur? What exactly would you do?

Are you afraid that you'd be devastated and overcome with painful emotion? Remember that we human beings are capable of enduring even the deepest of emotional pain. Sometimes we even manage to find meaning in it. Many people have persevered through amazing adversity over the course of human history. But our modern culture seems to teach us that tragedies should never happen. We expect to get through life unscathed and consider ourselves to have failed if tragedy does strike. Allow yourself to feel vulnerable as you face this possible scenario. If the worst did happen, you wouldn't get over it right away—maybe your life would never be the same. But you could still go on and create a meaningful life, probably in ways you can't even imagine.

Safety worries often take hold when you see yourself as responsible for everything and everyone around you. Carefully examine any beliefs that you're responsible for anticipating everything under the sun and preventing any conceivable disaster. You might expect to control everything that could possibly happen in the future, all the while knowing deep down that this is impossible. You wind up feeling hopeless and eventually swing to the other extreme, believing that you're completely powerless. Both of these extremes— either seeing yourself as helpless and completely ruled by your surroundings or believing you have an absolute power to control everything—can fuel safety worry spirals.

Step 5: Explore New Perspectives

As you explore new perspectives, check for any hidden beliefs about the benefits of worrying about safety. Do you still think your worry will prevent something tragic from happening because you're constantly on guard? How attentive to the world around you can you really be if your mind is off in the future, caught up in worry? Compare times in which you were worried to times in which you were really living in the present moment. Aren't you best able to respond to your surroundings when you're fully tuned into what's going on around you at that moment?

Be sure to explore the disadvantages of holding onto your safety worries. If you're a mother worrying about the safety of your children, are you missing out on the joy of raising them? After all, this is the main reason many women want to have children in the first place. Remember that there are limits to our ability to control the future. You can choose to accept these limits and be willing to face whatever life throws your way instead of worrying your life away with illusions of all-powerful control.

FACE YOUR FEARS

In chapter 5 you learned to confront the things you avoid in a gradual way. What activities or situations have you avoided because of your safety worries? Maybe you sometimes avoid watching, reading, or listening to the news. But also look for less apparent things, such as hearing or talking about tragedies. Do you change the subject when your friends are discussing such topics? Do you avoid watching movies in which death or disaster is part of the plot? As you gradually start to face these situations, allow yourself to feel the vulnerability that comes from being in touch with your own mortality.

Also look for any subtle worry spiral behaviors you might do in response to your safety worry. Do you repeatedly call loved ones to make sure that they're safe? If you're a mother, are you a bit overprotective with your children, not allowing them to do activities all their friends are permitted to do? Be careful about accidentally teaching your kids that the world is a dangerous and scary place—children are very perceptive and pick up a lot of our behaviors and fears just by watching us. Whenever you're tempted to do these worry behaviors as part of a safety worry spiral, challenge yourself to do something different instead.

RELAX YOUR BODY AND MIND

You learned some specific ways to relax in chapter 6. Safety worries can lead to an anxious and tense body quite quickly. As you continue to monitor your worry spirals, notice how your body reacts to these worries. Check in with your breathing and see if it has become fast and shallow—this is a cue to take a moment and practice your deep breathing. Are you picking up on any extra muscle tension that you don't need? Relax this tension away while breathing slowly and deeply when you catch yourself worrying about safety. Then when you have more time, examine these worries carefully and take action to face these fears directly.

FOCUS ON THE PRESENT MOMENT

As you catch your worry about safety and apply your relaxation techniques, be sure to bring your mind back to the present moment. Remember, we are best able to react to the world around us when we're paying full attention in the here and now. Experience all the feelings that come from being fully present right in this moment. Notice any feelings of gratitude and appreciation for all that you do have and cherish. If you worry about the safety of a loved one, how do you feel about having that person in your life *right now* in this particular moment? This question can help you shift gears from worrying about what could happen to your loved one to feeling joy that you have that person in your life right now.

Gain a New Perspective

Get Specific

- Can you take any specific action?

Generate Alternatives

- Include less dramatic possibilities.

Look at the Evidence

- It's not more likely to happen just because you're thinking about it.

- Don't misinterpret images or emotions as evidence that it's likely.

Suppose the Worst Did Happen

- You can cope with adversity.

Explore New Perspectives

- Let go of hidden beliefs about the benefits of this worry.

Face Your Fears

- Stop avoiding conversations or movies about tragic events.

- Give up overly cautious worry spiral behaviors.

Relax Your Body and Mind

- Let go of muscle tension and shift to deep breathing.

Focus on the Present Moment

- Refocus on the joy of the current moment.

CHAPTER 11

Final Thoughts

Hopefully you've learned some useful information about worry and discovered new ways of responding to it. If you worry about relationships, work, or safety, you also learned how to tailor your coping strategies to these specific topics. But what if you worry about little things that don't fall neatly into any of these categories? Many women get caught up with worry about small stuff, the everyday hassles we all face: being late for an appointment, making sure the kids are ready for school, finding a parking space, getting the car repaired, preparing dinner, and making sure homework gets done. If you worry about minor things, go ahead and practice the strategies you learned in part 2. Eventually, you can take a shortcut and quickly put these worries into perspective by asking yourself a few key questions:

- So what if this does happen?

- Why would this be such a big deal?

- How important is this compared to what matters most in my life?

Compare the importance of your minor worries to the things in your life you care most about. If it helps, you could even write a list of what's most important to you. Then you can shift your attention back to what you really value, getting in touch with any feelings of joy and gratitude that come up. This makes letting go of the small stuff a bit easier.

You've already taken a big step forward just by reading this book. Remember that you have the power to enrich your life and turn your old worry spiral habits around. Best of luck as you keep up your practice and continue down your own unique path of self-discovery!

Resources

HOW TO FIND A THERAPIST

Most therapists trained in the type of therapy described in this book are licensed psychologists with a Ph.D. degree. A couple of well-respected organizations have free referral services on their Web sites. Use these Web sites to find a psychologist in your geographical area:

Anxiety Disorders Association of America—www.adaa.org

Association for Advancement of Behavior Therapy—
www.aabt.org

ADDITIONAL READING
Panic and Phobias

Antony, M. 1995. *Mastery of Your Specific Phobia: Client Workbook*. Boulder, Colo.: Graywind Publications.

Antony, M., and R. McCabe. 2004. *10 Simple Solutions to Panic: How to Overcome Panic Attacks, Calm Physical Symptoms, and Reclaim Your Life.* Oakland, Calif.: New Harbinger Publications.

Barlow, D., and M. Craske. 2000. *Mastery of Your Anxiety and Panic: Client Workbook (MAP-3)*, 3rd ed. San Antonio, Tex.: Psychological Corporation.

Bourne, E. 2005. *The Anxiety and Phobia Workbook*, 4th ed. Oakland, Calif.: New Harbinger Publications.

Brown, D. 1996. *Flying without Fear.* Oakland, Calif.: New Harbinger Publications.

Pollard, C. A., and E. Zuercher-White. 2003. *The Agoraphobia Workbook: A Comprehensive Program to End Your Fear of Symptom Attacks.* Oakland, Calif.: New Harbinger Publications.

Zuercher-White, E. 1998. *An End to Panic: Breakthrough Techniques for Overcoming Panic Disorder.* Oakland, Calif.: New Harbinger Publications.

Shyness and Social Anxiety

Antony, M. 2004. *10 Simple Solutions to Shyness.* Oakland, Calif.: New Harbinger Publications.

Antony, M., and R. Swinson. 2000. *The Shyness and Social Anxiety Workbook: Proven Techniques for Overcoming Your Fears.* Oakland, Calif.: New Harbinger Publications.

Hope, D., R. Heimberg, H. Juster, and C. Turk. 2000. *Managing Social Anxiety: A Cognitive-Behavioral Therapy Approach.* San Antonio, Tex.: Psychological Corporation.

Markway, B., C. Carmin, C. A. Pollard, and T. Flynn. 1992. *Dying of Embarrassment: Help for Social Anxiety and Social Phobia.* Oakland, Calif.: New Harbinger Publications.

Stein, M., and J. Walker. 2002. *Triumph Over Shyness: Conquering Shyness and Social Anxiety.* New York: McGraw-Hill.

Health Anxiety

Zgourides, G. 2002. *Stop Worrying about Your Health! How to Quit Obsessing about Symptoms and Feel Better Now.* Oakland, Calif.: New Harbinger Publications.

Depression

Addis, M., and C. Martell. 2004. *Overcoming Depression One Step at a Time: The New Behavioral Activation Approach to Getting Your Life Back.* Oakland, Calif.: New Harbinger Publications.

Bieling, P., and M. Antony. 2003. *Ending the Depression Cycle: A Step-by-Step Guide for Preventing Relapse.* Oakland, Calif.: New Harbinger Publications.

Burns, D. 1999. *Feeling Good: The New Mood Therapy.* New York: Avon Books.

Nolen-Hoeksema, S. 2003. *Women Who Think Too Much: How to Break Free of Overthinking and Reclaim Your Life.* New York: Henry Holt and Company.

Mindfulness Practice

Albers, S. 2003. *Eating Mindfully: How to End Mindless Eating and Enjoy a Balanced Relationship with Food.* Oakland, Calif.: New Harbinger Publications.

Brantley, J. 2003. *Calming Your Anxious Mind: How Mindfulness and Compassion Can Free You from Anxiety, Fear, and Panic.* Oakland, Calif.: New Harbinger Publications.

Kabat-Zinn, J. 1990. *Full Catastrophe Living.* New York: Dell Publishing.

Kabat-Zinn, J. 1994. *Wherever You Go, There You Are.* New York: Hyperion.

Resources

Sex and Communication

Foley, S., S. Kope, and D. Sugrue. 2002. *Sex Matters for Women: A Complete Guide to Taking Care of Your Sexual Self.* New York: Guilford Press.

Zoldbrod, A., and L. Dockett. 2002. *Sex Talk: Uncensored Exercises for Exploring What Really Turns You On.* Oakland, Calif.: New Harbinger Publications.

References

Anxiety Disorders Association of America. 2003. Statistics and Facts about Anxiety Disorders. www.adaa.org/media room/index.cfm.

Arcus, D., and J. Kagan. 1995. Temperament and craniofacial variation in the first two years. *Child Development* 66(5):1529-1540.

Bernstein, D., and T. Borkovec. 1973. *Progressive Relaxation Training: A Manual for the Helping Professions.* Champaign, Ill.: Research Press.

Bernstein, D., T. Borkovec, and H. Hazlett-Stevens. 2000. *New Directions in Progressive Relaxation Training: A Guidebook for Helping Professionals.* Westport, Conn.: Praeger Publishers.

Borkovec, T., M. Newman, A. Pincus, and R. Lytle. 2002. A component analysis of cognitive behavioral therapy for generalized anxiety disorder and the role of interpersonal problems. *Journal of Consulting and Clinical Psychology* 70:288–298.

Borkovec, T., and A. Ruscio. 2001. Psychotherapy for generalized anxiety disorder. *Journal of Clinical Psychiatry* 62 (Suppl. 11):37–45.

Borysenko, J. 1996. *A Woman's Book of Life: The Biology, Psychology, and Spirituality of the Feminine Life Cycle.* New York: Putnam.

Brown, T., T. O'Leary, and D. Barlow. 2001. Generalized anxiety disorder. In *Clinical Handbook of Psychological Disorders,* third edition, ed. D. Barlow (pp. 154-208). New York: Guilford Press.

Craske, M. G. 2003. *Origins of Phobias and Anxiety Disorders: Why More Women Than Men?* Oxford: Elsevier Press.

Dugas, M., M. Freeston, and R. Ladouceur. 1997. Intolerance of uncertainty and problem orientation in worry. *Cognitive Therapy and Research* 21:593–606.

Gould, R., S. Safren, D. Washington, and M. Otto. 2004. A meta-analytic review of cognitive-behavioral treatments. In *Generalized Anxiety Disorder: Advances in Research and Practice,* ed. R. Heimberg, C. Turk, and D. Mennin (pp. 248–264). New York: Guilford Press.

Hazlett-Stevens, H., and M. Craske. 2003. The catastrophizing worry process in generalized anxiety disorder: A preliminary investigation of an analog population. *Behavioural and Cognitive Psychotherapy* 31:387–401.

Jacobson, E. 1938. *Progressive Relaxation.* Chicago: University of Chicago Press.

Kabat-Zinn, J., A. Massion, J. Kristeller, L. Peterson, K. Fletcher, L. Pbert, W. Lenderking, and S. Santorelli. 1992. Effectiveness of a meditation-based stress reduction program in the treatment of anxiety disorders. *American Journal of Psychiatry* 149:936–943.

Lynn, R., and T. Martin. 1997. Gender differences in extraversion, neuroticism, and psychoticism in 37 nations. *Journal of Social Psychology* 137(3):369–373.

McGee, R., M. Feehan, S. Williams, and J. Anderson. 1992. DSM-III disorders from age 11 to age 15 years. *Journal of* the *American Academy of Child and Adolescent Psychiatry* 31:50–59.

Meyer, T., M. Miller, R. Metzger, and T. D. Borkovec. 1990. Development and validation of the Penn State Worry Questionnaire. *Behaviour Research and Therapy* 28:487-495.

Mor, N., and J. Winquist. 2002. Self-focused attention and negative affect: A meta-analysis. *Psychological Bulletin* 128(4):638–662.

Offord, D. R., M. H. Boyle, D. Campbell, P. Goering, E. Lin, M. Wong, and Y. Racine. 1996. One-year prevalence of psychiatric disorder in Ontarians 15 to 64 years of age. *Canadian Journal of Psychiatry* 41(9):559–563.

Ohannessian, C. M., R. M. Lerner, J. V. Lerner, and A. Eye. 1999. Does self-competence predict gender differences in adolescent depression and anxiety? *Journal of Adolescence* 22(3):397–411.

Orsillo, S., L. Roemer, and D. Barlow. 2003. Integrating acceptance and mindfulness into existing cognitive-behavioral treatment for GAD: A case study. *Cognitive and Behavioral Practice* 10:222–230.

Pennebaker, J. W. 2000. Psychological factors influencing the reporting of physical symptoms. In *The Science of Self-Report: Implications for Research and Practice*, ed. A. A. Stone and J. S. Turkkan (pp. 299-315). Mahwah, N.J.: Lawrence Erlbaum Associates.

Pennebaker, J. W., and T. Roberts. 1992. Toward a his and hers theory of emotion: Gender differences in visceral perception. *Journal of Social and Clinical Psychology* 11(3):199-212.

Rachman, S. 1990. *Fear and Courage*. San Francisco: W. H. Freeman & Co.

Roemer, L., S. Molina, and T. Borkovec. 1997. An investigation of worry content among generally anxious individuals. *Journal of Nervous and Mental Disease* 185:314–319.

Ruscio, A. 2002. Delimiting the boundaries of generalized anxiety disorder: Differentiating high worriers with and without GAD. *Journal of Anxiety Disorders* 16:377–400.

Wegner, D. 1989. *White Bears and Other Unwanted Thoughts.* New York: Guilford Press.

Wittchen, H., S. Zhao, R. Kessler, and W. Eaton. 1994. DSM-III-R generalized anxiety disorder in the National Comorbidity Survey. *Archives of General Psychiatry* 51:355–364.

Zinbarg, R., M. Craske, and D. Barlow. 1993. *Mastery of Your Anxiety and Worry: Therapist Guide.* Boulder, Colo.: Graywind Publications.

Holly Hazlett-Stevens, Ph.D., is assistant professor of psychology at the University of Nevada in Reno, NV. She has conducted psychological research in the areas of worry, anxiety, and relaxation for the past ten years, which has led to the publication of more than twenty journal articles and book chapters. She is coauthor of *New Directions in Progressive Relaxation Training*.

Michelle G. Craske, Ph.D., is professor of psychology and of psychiatry and biobehavioral sciences at the University of California, Los Angeles, and director of the UCLA Anxiety Disorders Behavioral Research Program. She has published over 100 articles and chapters in the areas of anxiety disorders and fear and is author of *Anxiety Disorders: Psychological Approaches to Theory and Treatment* and *Treatment and Origins of Phobias and Anxiety Disorders: Why More Women than Men?*

Some Other New Harbinger Titles

The Well-Ordered Office, Item 3856 $13.95

Talk to Me, Item 3317 $12.95

Romantic Intelligence, Item 3309 $15.95

Transformational Divorce, Item 3414 $13.95

The Rape Recovery Handbook, Item 3376 $15.95

Eating Mindfully, Item 3503 $13.95

Sex Talk, Item 2868 $12.95

Everyday Adventures for the Soul, Item 2981 $11.95

A Woman's Addiction Workbook, Item 2973 $18.95

The Daughter-In-Law's Survival Guide, Item 2817 $12.95

PMDD, Item 2833 $13.95

The Vulvodynia Survival Guide, Item 2914 $15.95

Love Tune-Ups, Item 2744 $10.95

The Deepest Blue, Item 2531 $13.95

The 50 Best Ways to Simplify Your Life, Item 2558 $11.95

Brave New You, Item 2590 $13.95

Loving Your Teenage Daughter, Item 2620 $14.95

The Hidden Feelings of Motherhood, Item 2485 $14.95

The Woman's Book of Sleep, Item 2493 $14.95

Pregnancy Stories, Item 2361 $14.95

The Women's Guide to Total Self-Esteem, Item 2418 $13.95

Thinking Pregnant, Item 2302 $13.95

The Conscious Bride, Item 2132 $12.95

Call **toll free, 1-800-748-6273,** or log on to our online bookstore at **www.newharbinger.com** to order. Have your Visa or Mastercard number ready. Or send a check for the titles you want to New Harbinger Publications, Inc., 5674 Shattuck Ave., Oakland, CA 94609. Include $4.50 for the first book and 75¢ for each additional book, to cover shipping and handling. (California residents please include appropriate sales tax.) Allow two to five weeks for delivery.

Prices subject to change without notice.